Pocket Rough Guide

# MARRAKESH

written and researched by

## DANIEL JACOBS

# Contents

# INTRODUCTION TO

# MARRAKESH

The last few years have seen Marrakesh well and truly established as Morocco's capital of chic, attracting the rich and famous from Europe and beyond. Yet the city has always had a mystique about it. It's a place of immense beauty, sitting beneath the dramatic peaks of the High Atlas mountains – its narrow alleys beg discovery while its thoroughfares bustle with excitement and vitality. Arguably the last outpost of the Mediterranean before the Sahara, Marrakesh is still steeped in nomadic and West African influences. Nowhere is this fact more evident than in the Jemaa el Fna, the main square at the heart of the old town. Here you'll find a constant reminder that Marrakesh was once the entrepôt for goods (gold, ivory and slaves) brought by caravan across the desert.

LANTERN SHOPPING IN THE SOUKS

## Best places for a mint tea

Top spots for a refreshing cup of Moroccan mint tea (*atai bi-nana*) include the **Grand Balcon** (see p.39), overlooking the Jemaa el Fna, and the **Café des Épices** (see p.56), overlooking the Rahba Kedima. When you're shopping in the souks, **Le Bougainvillier** (see p.56) is a beautiful place to take a breather for tea or a verbena infusion.

Like all Moroccan cities, Marrakesh is a town of two halves: the ancient walled Medina, founded by Sultan Youssef Ben Tachfine back in the Middle Ages, and the colonial Ville Nouvelle, built by the French in the early twentieth century. Each has its own delights – the Medina with its ancient palaces and mansions, labyrinthine souks and deeply traditional way of life; and the Ville Nouvelle with its pavement cafés, trendy shops, gardens and boulevards.

Marrakesh is sometimes called the Red City, and it won't take you long to see why. The natural red ochre pigment that bedecks its walls and buildings can at times seem dominant, but there's no shortage of other colours – there are few cities as vibrant as this one. Marrakesh breathes the scents of the Middle East and Africa: of spices, incense, and fresh wood being cut and crafted in workshops on the street. Yet simultaneously it oozes a French-inspired elegance in its cool riads, haute cuisine, stylish boutiques and gorgeous clothes. Whatever the wider influences, Marrakesh is first and foremost a Moroccan city, basking in a unique combination of Arab and Berber culture, which infuses its architecture, its craftwork, its cooking and its people.

For visitors, the Jemaa el Fna is undoubtedly the focus, a place without parallel in the world; really no more than an open space, it's also the stage for a long-established ritual in which shifting circles of onlookers gather round groups of acrobats, musicians, dancers, storytellers, comedians and fairground acts. It is always compelling, no matter how many times you return.

## When to visit

Weatherwise, **spring** (March–May) and **autumn** (Sept–Nov) are the best times to visit Marrakesh – it'll be sunny but not too hot. At the height of **summer** (June–Aug), daytime temperatures regularly reach a roasting 38ºC, and don't fall below a sweaty 20ºC at night, while in **winter** (Dec–Feb) the temperature may reach a pleasant 18ºC by day, but it can be grey and even wet; after dark, it's not unusual for temperatures to drop to just 4ºC or below. If you come in June or July, you can catch the Festival National des Arts Populaires with its musicians and nightly equestrian "fantasia", while late November or early December is the time to catch Marrakesh's film festival. Expect **accommodation** to be much in demand at Easter and at Christmas, when you should book well ahead and expect extra-high prices.

Away from the Jemaa, the rest of the Medina is a maze of irregular streets and alleys; losing yourself among them is one of the great pleasures of a visit to Marrakesh. Within the Medina's twelfth-century walls you'll find a profusion of mosques, Koranic schools and *zaouias* (tombs of holy men and women), amid what is, for most Western visitors, an exotic street life, replete with itinerant knife-grinders and fruit sellers, mules bearing heavy goods through the narrow thoroughfares, and country people in town to sell wares spread out upon the ground.

When you need a break from the bustle of the city streets, you can make for the peaks and valleys of the High Atlas mountains, a couple of hours' drive away, where wild flowers dot pastoral landscapes beneath the rugged wildness of sheer rock and snow. And just three hours away on the coast is the friendly, picturesque walled town of Essaouira. It's a centre for fine art as much as water sports, not to mention some excellent seafood dining.

MINZAH PAVILION, MENARA GARDENS

# MARRAKESH AT A GLANCE

## >> EATING

The most atmospheric place to eat is at the food stalls on the **Jemaa el Fna**, right in the middle of the action, but if you don't fancy mucking in at street level, there are also several decent, moderately priced restaurants overlooking the square. Inexpensive café-restaurants are concentrated in the streets just south of the Jemaa, and scattered around the **Medina** are some excellent upmarket palace-restaurants, usually with a floorshow in the evenings. These are often hidden away, and can be difficult to find, especially at night – if in doubt, phone in advance and ask for directions; sometimes the restaurant will send someone to meet you. Most of the city's French-style cafés, bistros and restaurants, many of which are very good, are to be found in the **Guéliz** district in the centre of the Ville Nouvelle, where there's a smattering of restaurants offering cuisine from further afield too. Only the more expensive places in the Medina serve **alcohol**, but in the Ville Nouvelle all but the cheapest places are licensed.

## >> SHOPPING

The **souk (market)** area in the northern half of the Medina is crammed with little shops selling crafts and clothing, as well as workshops where many of the items are made, and a wander round the souks is one of the highlights of any trip to Marrakesh. Before setting off into the souks, it's worth taking a look at the Ensemble Artisanal, or a fixed-price shop such as Entreprise Bouchaib, to get an idea of quality and prices. Parts of the souk, and other locations in the Medina, specialize in specific items: **carpets** in the Souk des Tapis, for example; **babouches** (Moroccan slippers) in Souk Smata; and **lanterns** in Place des Ferblantiers. Other specialities include **Morocco leather**, which is cured in the local tanneries, and local **clothes**, some of which are targeted particularly towards Western tastes. For **wooden marquetry**, Essaouira is the place to go. In most places, of course, you'll have to **haggle** – see p.125 for advice.

## >> DRINKING AND NIGHTLIFE

As an almost entirely Muslim city, Marrakesh doesn't have a big drinking culture. **Bars** tend to be either chic and sophisticated or rough and low-life (these can be fun, but for men more than for women), and there's not much in between. Most bars are in the Ville Nouvelle, with much more limited choice in the Medina. The city does have some quite decent **nightclubs**, all of them in the Ville Nouvelle, and mostly attached to five-star hotels. They play a mix of Western and Arabic music, but it's the latter that really fills the dancefloor.

**OUR RECOMMENDATIONS FOR WHERE TO EAT, DRINK AND SHOP ARE LISTED AT THE END OF EACH PLACES CHAPTER.**

# **Day One** in Marrakesh

**1 Jemaa el Fna** > p.34. Start out from Marrakesh's main square, just as it gets going in the morning.

**2 Souks** > p.44. Make for the souk area north of the Jemaa, where Marrakesh's vibrant markets are concentrated.

**3 Place de la Kissaria** > p.48. Pay a visit to the Marrakesh Museum, and have a look at the Almoravid Koubba while you're passing.

**4 Ben Youssef Medersa** > p.48. The most impressive medieval Koranic school in Morocco, with zellij tilework, intricate stucco and finely carved cedarwood.

**Lunch** > p.59. *Le Foundouk* is housed in an old caravanserai, and is now a stylish restaurant (closed on Mon).

**5 The Tanneries** > p.51. Head east to the stinky tanneries, checking them out at ground level and then from a roof terrace.

**6 Zaouia of Sidi Bel Abbes** > p.52. Go past Chrob ou Chouf fountain to the *zaouia*, or tomb, of Sidi Bel Abbes, the most important of Marrakesh's "seven saints".

**7 The Majorelle Garden** > p.72. Leave the Medina for the Ville Nouvelle's most important sight, a wonderful ornamental garden with cacti and lily ponds.

**Dinner** > p.80 & p.87. Dine on excellent Fassi cuisine at *Al Fassia* including pastilla and a choice of succulent lamb tajines. Advance booking is wise. Later, you might head to *Theatro* for some dancing.

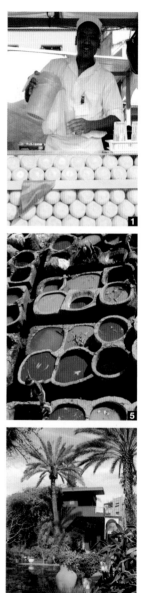

# Day Two in Marrakesh

**1 Bab Agnaou** > p.66. Begin at Marrakesh's most magnificent city gate, featuring concentric arches and fine carving. It also has a patisserie right inside it.

**2 The Saadian Tombs** > p.66. Arrive early to avoid the crowds (the enclosure opens at 9am) so you can appreciate the exquisite tombs at their best.

**3 Place des Ferblantiers** > p.61. Head to Place des Ferblantiers to watch the metalworkers beating out decorative lanterns by hand.

**4 El Badi Palace** > p.64. Take some time to explore this extensive and extremely impressive ruin, with its sunken gardens and pavilions.

**(🍴) Lunch** > p.69. Pause at the *Café el Badia*, where you can opt for a cheap set menu and get right up close to the storks nesting on the walls of the palace.

**5 Bahia Palace** > p.61. This nineteenth-century grand vizier's palace contains some of the city's finest painted ceilings.

**6 Dar Si Said** > p.60. Stop off at this nineteenth-century mansion, now a museum, to admire the woodwork and costumes.

**7 Jemaa el Fna** > p.34. The Jemaa el Fna should now be warming up for the evening, with snake charmers giving way to storytellers and musicians.

**(🍴) Dinner** > p.34 & p.57. Have supper at the food stalls on the Jemaa. Afterwards, head to the *Café Arabe* for a drink.

# Marrakesh's **souks**

In the medieval Medina, every craft had its own souk, or market, where artisans wrought and sold their products – a tradition that continues today.

**1 Souk Smarine** > p.44. This is the souks' main thoroughfare, where shafts of sunlight through the slatted roofs dapple the street below.

**2 Rahba Kedima** > p.45. An open square whose apothecary stalls sell all manner of strange traditional cosmetics.

**3 La Criée Berbère** > p.45. Once the site for slave auctions, this covered area now specializes in rugs and carpets.

**4 The Kissaria** > p.45. The covered market at the very heart of the souks, where clothes and fabrics dominate.

**Lunch** > p.59. Dine on Moroccan dishes with a modern twist up on the terrace of the *Terrasse des Épices*, with views across the rooftops.

**5 Souk Smata** > p.53. Also called the Souk des Babouches, this is where the slipper-makers ply their wares.

**6 Souk Haddadine** > p.48. The ironworkers' souk is a cacophony of clanging as the craftsmen hammer out their metal.

**7 Souk Sabbaghine** > p.45. Here in the dyers' souk, plain wool is boiled up in vats of luridly tinted liquids and hung out to dry across the street and the rooftops.

**Dinner** > p.58. Try *La Maison Arabe* for a really top-notch Moroccan meal in elegant surroundings.

# Indulgent Marrakesh

Marrakesh is Morocco's indisputable capital of chic, so there's no better place for a spot of pampering.

**1 Breakfast at the Patisserie des Princes** > p.39. Set yourself up for the day with coffee, croissants and maybe even a pastry.

**2 A calèche ride in the Palmery** > p.75. Sit back in a horse-drawn carriage and ride in style through Marrakesh's oasis.

**3 Ice cream at Oliveri** > p.80. Pop into this elegant salon to eat the city's best ice cream in old-fashioned style.

**4 Shop in the Ville Nouvelle** > p.76. Check out fine antiques, home furnishings and sumptuous Morocco leather.

**Lunch** > p.81. Head to the *Grand Café de la Poste* for fine international cuisine in a classic restaurant.

**5 Get a henna tattoo in the Jemaa el Fna** > p.35. Have your hands decorated with the same designs as a Moroccan bride.

**6 Mint tea at La Mamounia** > p.39. Take tea on the terrace and enjoy the royal gardens.

**7 A steam bath at Les Bains de Marrakech** > p.111. Book the full package, with steam bath, massage, mud packs and all the extras.

**Dinner** > p.42 & p.81. Have supper at *Le Tobsil*, where the pastilla and the couscous are second to none. Advance booking is essential. Then pop into the *Comptoir Darna* for a post-prandial cocktail.

BEST OF MARRAKESH

# Big sights

**1 Jemaa el Fna** The heart and soul of the city, and an absolutely unmatchable experience after nightfall. > **p.34**

**2 El Badi Palace** Morocco's most fascinating ruin, the remains of a huge, rambling palace with pavilions and formal gardens. > **p.64**

**3 Majorelle Garden** One of the world's great gardens, created by a French artist in the early twentieth century. > **p.72**

**4 Koutoubia** The ultimate masterpiece of Almohad architecture, perfectly proportioned and breathtakingly beautiful – the city's emblem. > **p.36**

**5 Ben Youssef Medersa** A medieval Koranic school where you'll find the city's finest examples of tilework, stucco and carved cedarwood. > **p.48**

15

# Museums and galleries

**1 Maison Tiskiwin** A unique collection of artefacts harking back to the days of the trans-Saharan caravan trade between Morocco and Mali. > **p.60**

**2 Dar Si Said** This gorgeous mansion now houses a superb collection of furniture and carved cedarwood. > **p.60**

**3 Galerie d'Art Frederic Damgaard** The top gallery in Essaouira displays the town's own distinctive style of painting and sculpture. > **p.98**

**4 Marrakesh Museum** This imposing nineteenth-century politician's mansion now houses exhibitions of Moroccan art and sculpture. > **p.48**

**5 La Qoubba Galerie** New work by local artists is displayed at this little gallery attached to the tomb of a saint. > **p.55**

# Shopping

**1 Carpets** Knotted or woven, large or small, you'll find carpets from all over southern Morocco at shops like Bazar de Sud in La Criée Berbère, the carpet souk. > **p.45 & p.53**

**2 Thuya marquetry** Essaouira is the place to buy items made from the wood and root of the thuya tree, often inlaid with other woods. > **p.97**

**3 Babouches** Traditional Moroccan slippers, in a profusion of styles – see them being made by hand at El Louami Ahmed. > **p.68**

**4 Tyre crafts** Used car and bicycle tyres are turned into kitsch but appealing items at Cadre en Pneus, among others. > **p.67**

**5 Knitted caps** Brightly coloured skullcaps – you'll need short hair to wear them – are a big favourite with Moroccan men. Find them in the Souk Smarine. > **p.44**

# Religious Marrakesh

**1** **The Kasbah Mosque** The main mosque of the citadel quarter has been restored to look as it did in its heyday. > **p.66**

**2 Église des Saints-Martyrs**
Marrakesh's red-ochre Catholic church is a remnant of French colonial rule. > **p.74**

**3 Lazama Synagogue** The most important synagogue in Marrakesh's Mellah, or Jewish quarter, is located inside a private house. > **p.64**

**4 Almoravid Koubba** Morocco's only surviving Almoravid building shows how many typical motifs are Almoravid in origin. > **p.48**

**5 Zaouia of Sidi Bel Abbes** This shrine is a sanctuary for Marrakesh's blind, dedicated to their patron saint. > **p.52**

# Food

**1 Tajine** Slow-cooked until sumptuously tender, Morocco's signature dish is served at any cheap diner, but it's best at top-class restaurants like *Al Fassia*. > **p.80**

**2 Sweets** Sticky with syrup and stuffed with nuts, Moroccan pastries are sold in the heart of the Medina at *Patisserie Belkabir*. > **p.57**

**3 Couscous** Berber in origin, this is the classic North African dish: steamed semolina pellets, moist and aromatic. Try it at *Le Tobsil*. > **p.42**

**4 Tanjia** Jugged beef or lamb, this is Marrakesh's speciality; eat it with the locals at places like *Hadj Mustapha*, just off Souk Ableuh. > **p.41**

**5 Pastilla** Sweet pigeon pie from Fez, now available in seafood or even vegetarian versions. *La Maison Arabe* does the best pastilla in town. > **p.58**

# Riads

**1 Riyad al Moussika** A sumptuous blend of Moroccan artistry and Italian panache, where classical music plays and the food is exquisite. **> p.113**

**2 Riad Star** Experience the luxurious atmosphere of the newest and the most vibrant riad in the city. **> p.110**

**4 Noir d'Ivoire** The black, brown and cream colour scheme oozes style – a place to indulge yourself. **> p.108**

**3 Riad Elizabeth** A fun, British-run riad, not chic but certainly stylish, with snazzy, mirror-tiled disco loos. **> p.108**

**5 Riad Kniza** If you want a top-notch but totally Moroccan experience, this is the riad to come to. **> p.109**

# Bars and nightlife

**1 Chesterfield Pub** This may be an approximation to an English pub but it's also rather more sophisticated, serving cocktails rather than pints. > **p.85**

**2 Pacha** A branch of the famous Ibiza rave club, this is Marrakesh's most exciting nightspot. **> p.87**

**3 Comptoir Darna** A fine restaurant and excellent bar, and also one of the city's most popular nightlife spots. **> p.81**

**4 So Night Lounge** Dress to kill if you want to get into Marrakesh's hippest and most exclusive nightclub, a super-cool lounge bar, with multiple dancefloors and even tables to dine at. **> p.87**

**5 The Jemaa el Fna by night** For atmosphere, you can't beat dining under the stars to the accompaniment of rhythmic Gnaoua music. **> p.41**

# Sports and activities

**1** **Skiing at Oukaïmeden** Twenty kilometres of runs for skiers and snowboarders in the snowy High Atlas mountains, two hours from town. **> p.90**

## 2 Trekking in the Atlas

Crystalline mountain air, snowy peaks and green valleys await trekkers and hikers in the High Atlas mountains. > **p.89**

## 3 Windsurfing in Essaouira

Morocco's top windsurfing spot, where reliable winds ensure some of the best sailboarding in North Africa. > **p.96**

**4 Golf** Morocco has some top-class courses, including three excellent ones around Marrakesh, with the Atlas mountains for a backdrop. > **p.124**

**5 Camel riding** Pop up to the Palmery to climb onto a camel and be Lawrence of Arabia for the afternoon. > **p.75**

# Festivals and events

**1 Essaouira Gnaoua Festival** A celebration of music from the unique Sufi sect originally formed by slaves from West Africa. **> p.96**

**2 Festival National des Arts Populaires** Singing, dancing, camel racing and an equestrian "fantasia" feature in this week-long festival in June or July. > **p.130**

**3 Moussem at Setti Fatma**
There are swaying Sufis, a fair and a market at this four-day traditional festival held every August. > **p.90**

**4 Ramadan** It's abstinence by day and partying by night throughout the holy month, when the fast is traditionally broken with a meal of dates and *harira* soup. > **p.130**

**5 Marrakesh Film Festival** Stars from Europe, the US and the Arab world gather in Marrakesh for this cinematic celebration. > **p.130**

PLACES

# The Jemaa el Fna and the Koutoubia

Once, every Moroccan city had a main square where story-tellers and musicians entertained the townspeople, but the Jemaa el Fna has always been the biggest and most important, drawing the greatest variety of performers, and it remains Morocco's single top attraction. To see why, come here as it gets going in the evening; you'll soon be squatting amid the onlookers, soaking in the unique atmosphere. For respite, the café and restaurant rooftop terraces set around it afford a view over the square and of the Koutoubia minaret – as much a symbol of Marrakesh as Big Ben is of London – while the northern edge of the square marks the beginning of Marrakesh's souks, or markets.

## JEMAA EL FNA

MAP P.36–37, POCKET MAP A12–B12

Nobody is entirely sure when or how the Jemaa el Fna came into being – or even what its name means. The usual translation is "assembly of the dead", which could refer to the public display here of the heads of rebels and criminals, since the Jemaa was a place of execution well into the nineteenth century.

By day, most of the square is just a big open space, in which a handful of **snake charmers** play their flutes at cruelly de-fanged cobras, **medicine men** (especially in the northeast of the square) display cures and nostrums and **tooth-pullers**, wielding fearsome pliers, offer to pluck the pain from out of the heads of toothache sufferers, trays of extracted molars attesting to their skill. It isn't

## Performers in the Jemaa el Fna

The locals' favourite among the square's performers are the **storytellers**, great raconteurs who draw quite a throng with their largely humorous tales, though of less interest to non-Arabic speakers of course. Also in attendance are **acrobats** and male **dancers in drag**. In the daytime, **monkey men** and **snake charmers** encourage tourists to pose for photos, but the animals are poached from the wild and treated cruelly, and paying for photos encourages this. Far better then to have your picture taken with the **tooth-pullers**, or the **water sellers** in their magnificent red regalia.

Dozens of musicians in the square play all kinds of instruments. In the evening there are full groups including **Gnaoua trance-healers**, members of a Sufi brotherhood of Senegalese origin, who beat out hour-long hypnotic rhythms with clanging iron castanets and pound tall drums with long curved sticks. Other groups play Moroccan popular folk music, known as *chaabi*, and late into the night, when almost everyone has gone home, you'll still find players plucking away at their lute-like *ginbris*.

until late afternoon that the crowds really build. At dusk, as in France and Spain, people come out for an early evening **promenade** (especially in Rue Bab Agnaou), and the square gradually fills with storytellers, acrobats and musicians (see box above), and the crowds who come to see them. Most of the spectators are Moroccan of course (few foreigners, for example, will understand the storytellers' tales), but tourists also contribute to both the atmosphere and the cashflow. There are sideshow attractions too: games of hoop-the-bottle; **fortune-tellers** sitting under umbrellas with packs of fortune-telling cards at the ready; and women with piping bags full of **henna** paste, ready

to paint hands, feet or arms with "tattoos". These will last up to three months, but beware of synthetic "black henna", which contains a toxic chemical; only red henna is natural.

For **refreshment**, stalls offer freshly squeezed orange and grapefruit juice, while neighbouring handcarts are piled high with dates, dried figs, almonds and walnuts, especially delicious in winter when they are freshly picked in the surrounding countryside.

As dusk falls, the square becomes a huge **open-air dining area** (see box, p.41), packed with stalls lit by gas lanterns, and the air is filled with wonderful smells and plumes of cooking smoke spiralling up into the night.

| RESTAURANTS | |
|---|---|
| Al Baraka | 10 |
| Chez Bahia | 16 |
| Chez Chegrouni | 5 |
| Earth Café | 22 |
| El Bahja | 21 |
| Hadj Mustapha | 2 |
| Hotel Islane | |
| Terrace Panoramique | 15 |
| Jemaa food stalls | 8 |
| Jnane Mogador | 20 |
| Kassabine Café | 1 |
| Le Marrakchi | 6 |
| Le Tobsil | 3 |
| Les Prémices | 13 |
| Pizzeria Portofino | 14 |
| Restaurant Argana | 4 |
| Restaurant Oscar Progrès | 23 |
| Taj'in Darna | 7 |

| ACCOMMODATION | |
|---|---|
| Hotel Aday | 8 |
| Hotel Ali | 2 |
| Hotel Central Palace | 3 |
| Hotel CTM | 1 |
| Hotel de Foucauld | 11 |
| Hotel Essaouira | 6 |
| Hotel Gallia | 12 |
| Hotel Ichbilia | 4 |
| Hotel La Mamounia | 13 |
| Hotel Medina | 5 |
| Hotel Sherazade | 10 |
| Jnane Mogador Hotel | 7 |
| Riad Zinoun | 9 |

*Map labels:* Bab Laksour; Ensemble Artesanal; RUE JEBEL LAKHDAR; RUE FATIMA ZOHRA; M'OULAY ABDELLAH BEN HESSAIEN; Tomb of Sidi Ali Bel Kacem; AVENUE MOHAMMED V; bus #6 (Agdal Gardens); Excavations; Koutoubia; Sidi Ali Bel Kacem Cemetery; Koutoubia Gardens; AVENUE HOUMAN EL FETOUAKI; Asni Shared Taxis; PLACE YOUSSEF TACHFINE; La Mamounia Hotel; Mamounia Gardens; bus #25 (Lagarb)

## THE KOUTOUBIA

MAP P.36–37, POCKET MAP F6

Rising dramatically from the palm trees to the west of the square, the **minaret** of the Koutoubia Mosque – nearly 70m high and visible for miles

– is the oldest of the three great towers built by Morocco's twelfth-century Almohad rulers (the others are the Hassan Tower in Rabat and the Giralda in Seville). The minaret's proportions give it an extraordinary lightness of feel, and its 1:5 ratio of width to height set the standard for minarets throughout Morocco. Indeed the Koutoubia displays many features that are now widespread in Moroccan architecture – the wide band of **ceramic inlay** near the top, the castellated **battlements** rising above it, the *darj w ktarf* ("cheek and shoulder" – similar to the French *fleur de lys*) – and the alternation of patterning on the different faces. At the summit are three great **copper balls**, thought to have been made originally of gold.

THE KOUTOUBIA

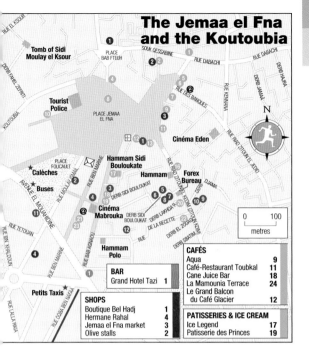

# The Jemaa el Fna and the Koutoubia

Tomb of Sidi Moulay el Ksour

PLACE BAB FTEUH

SOUK QESSABINE

RUE DABACHI

RUE DABACHI

RUE EL KSOUR

DERB FAREL ZERRITI

KOUTOUBIA

Tourist Police

PLACE JEMAA EL FNA

RUE DES BANQUES

Cinéma Eden

DERB JMAAI

DERB HLIRA

N

RUE RIAD ZITOUN EL JEDID

RUE KENNARIA

PLACE FOUCAULT

Calèches

Buses

AVENUE EL MOUAHIDINE

RUE TETOUAN

RUE BEN KHALDOUN

RUE BAB KENNOU

RUE BEN MARINE

RUE MOULAY ISMAIL

Hammam Sidi Boulokate

Hammam

DERB SIDI BOULOUKAT

Cinéma Mabrouka

DERB SIDI BOULOUKAT

DERB LAKHDA

DE LA RECETTE

RUE

Forex Bureau

RUE RIAD ZITOUN EL KEDIM (ZITOUN KDIM)

DJAMA

DERB EL ZOUAK

DERB EL ZOUAK

DERB SBATHI

0    100
metres

Hammam Polo

**BAR**
Grand Hotel Tazi    1

Petits Taxis

RUE LALLA RIKIA

RUE COBA BEN NAFAA

**SHOPS**
Boutique Bel Hadj    1
Hermane Rahal    4
Jemaa el Fna market    3
Olive stalls    2

**CAFÉS**
Aqua    9
Café-Restaurant Toubkal    11
Cane Juice Bar    18
La Mamounia Terrace    24
Le Grand Balcon
du Café Glacier    12

**PATISSERIES & ICE CREAM**
Ice Legend    17
Patisserie des Princes    19

Originally the minaret was covered with plaster and painted, like the Kasbah Mosque, near the Saadian Tombs (see p.66). In the evening, the minaret is floodlit to stunning effect.

To the north of the present-day mosque (which only Muslims may enter), you can see the remains of the original mosque, which predates it. The excavations confirm that the mosque had to be rebuilt to correct its alignment with Mecca.

## THE KOUTOUBIA GARDENS

Av Houman el Fetouaki. Daily 8am–6pm. MAP P.36–37, POCKET MAP E6–F6

To the south and west of the Koutoubia are the Koutoubia Gardens, attractively laid out with pools and fountains, roses, orange trees and palms. Something of a focus for

promenading Marrakshis, they give excellent views of the Koutoubia.

## LA MAMOUNIA HOTEL AND GARDENS

Av Bab Jedid. MAP P.36–37, POCKET MAP E6–F7

It's worth popping into Marrakesh's top hotel for a pot of tea on the terrace and a look at the opulent interior, with its 1920s Art Deco touches. The terrace overlooks the hotel's **gardens**, which regular visitor Winston Churchill described to Franklin D. Roosevelt when they were here together in 1943 as the loveliest spot in the world. Originally laid out by the Saadians, they retain the traditional elements of citrus trees and walkways. You'll have to dress up to see them, however, as jeans, shorts, trainers and T-shirts are all banned.

# Shops

## BOUTIQUE BEL HADJ

22 & 33 Souk Fondouk Louarzazi,
Place Bab Fteuh ☎ 0524 441258. Daily
10am–7pm. MAP P.36–37, POCKET MAP B11

If silver is your thing, this shop
on the north side of Place Bab
Fteuh is the place to look, with
heavy silver bracelets from
around Morocco and as far
afield as Afghanistan, sold by
weight and purity. There's other
silverware too – antique teapots
for example (often as not made
in Manchester for the Moroccan
market), along with tea trays.

## HERMANE RAHAL

3 Rue Moulay Ismail ☎ 0661 162535. Daily
10am–10pm. MAP P.36–37, POCKET MAP A13

Should you wish to buy a tajine
dish (see box, p.42), this
unassuming little store is the
place to do it. There are pretty
tajines here from Fez and Safi,
but the real McCoy are the
heavy red earthenware jobs
which hail from Sale on the
coast, where the local clay is
perfect for the purpose. A Sale

tajine will set you back 15–70dh,
depending on the size.

## JEMAA EL FNA MARKET

East side of Jemaa el Fna. Daily 9am–9pm.
MAP P.36–37, POCKET MAP B12

Just off the big square is this
small covered market, of most
interest as a place to get fruit
and veg, though it also sells
meat and even shoes. Handy if
you're staying in one of the
small hotels south of the Jemaa.

## OLIVE STALLS

Souk Ableuh. Daily 10am–8pm. MAP P.36–37,
POCKET MAP B12

Located in a little square just off
the Jemaa el Fna is a row of stalls
with olives piled up at the front.
The wrinkled black ones are the
typical Moroccan olive, delicious
with bread but a bit salty on
their own. As for the green
olives, the ones flavoured with
bits of lemon are among the
tastiest. Other delicacies include
spicy red *harissa* sauce and
bright yellow lemons preserved
in brine, the brine taking the
edge off the lemons' acidity.

# Cafés

## AQUA

66 Pl Jemaa el Fna ☎ 0526 887430. Daily
9am–midnight. MAP P.37

Cool, modern surrounds, and
two terraces overlooking the
western side of the Jemaa el
Fna. There are set breakfasts
(50–55dh), and espressos
made with an imported Italian
coffee blend, as well as
sandwiches, salads, juices and
pizzas, but the location and
ambience are more interesting
than the food.

## CAFÉ-RESTAURANT TOUBKAL

Southeast corner of Jemaa el Fna, by Rue
Riad Zitoun el Kedim. Daily 24hr. MAP P.36–37,
POCKET MAP B12

OLIVE STALL

As well as fruit juices, home-made yoghurts and pastries, they offer a range of salads, tajines and couscous here. It's also a great place for a breakfast of coffee with bread and jam or *msimmen* (a chewy, flat griddle bread) with honey. You'll be hard put to spend more than 70dh.

### LA MAMOUNIA TERRACE

Av Bab Jedid ☎ 0524 388600, Ⓦ mamounia .com. Daily 10am–7pm. MAP P.36–37, POCKET MAP E6

Dress up in proper shoes, and a skirt or trousers, to try the poshest cup of tea in town, served on the terrace of the *Hotel La Mamounia* (see p.37). The tea itself is nothing special, but it does allow you to check out the hotel's interior, and its beautiful gardens.

### LE GRAND BALCON DU CAFÉ GLACIER

South side of Jemaa el Fna, next to the Hotel CTM. Daily 10am–10pm (food served until 8pm). MAP P.36–37, POCKET MAP B12

This is the place for the fullest view over the Jemaa, taking it all in from a perfect vantage point, but it isn't as close-up as the *Restaurant Argana*. You can come up for just a drink (tea, coffee or soda) but they also do food, including salads, pizzas and tajines, with most dishes at 50–65dh.

### MAHALABAT QASAB ES SUKAR

38 Rue Bab Agnaou. Daily 7am–11pm. MAP P.36–37, POCKET MAP B13

This may be a standard coffee and juice bar at the back, but out front they sell "crêpes" (well, *msimmen*) stuffed with various sweet and savoury fillings for 5–12dh, and wonderful freshly pressed sugar cane juice (6dh a cup) – the only place in Marrakesh to sell it. Look for the juice machine as the sign is in Arabic only.

PATISSERIE DES PRINCES

# Patisseries and ice cream

## ICE LEGEND

Rue Bab Agnaou ☎ 0524 420320. Daily 10am–9pm. MAP P.36–37, POCKET MAP B12

The Marrakesh branch of this well-established Agadir ice-cream firm offers an eclectic range of over twenty flavours from blackcurrant or apricot sorbet to pecan, hazelnut and even licorice – heaven on a scorching day. From 7dh, but takeaway only.

## PATISSERIE DES PRINCES

32 Rue Bab Agnaou ☎ 0524 443033. Daily 6am–11pm. MAP P.36–37, POCKET MAP B13

*Patisserie des Princes* is a sparkling place that sells mouthwatering pastries at prices that are a little high by local standards but well worth the extra. They also have treats like almond milk and ice cream. The *salon de thé* at the back is a very civilized place to take a continental breakfast, morning coffee or afternoon tea.

# Restaurants

CHEZ BAHIA

### AL BARAKA

1 Pl Jemaa el Fna, by the Tourist Police
☎0524 442341, ✆albaraka-marrakech.com.
Daily noon–3pm & 7–10pm. MAP P.36–37,
POCKET MAP A12

This is a cool outdoor space
serving tasty meals (*menus*
320–450dh) accompanied in
the evening by a belly-dancing
show. Not in the same league as
some of the more palatial
Medina restaurants, and
something of a tourist trap, but
the food's good, the surroundings pleasant and the location
couldn't be handier. Licensed.

### CHEZ BAHIA

206 Rue Riad Zitoun el Kedim ☎0671 525224.
Daily 6am–midnight. MAP P.36–37, POCKET MAP B12

A café-diner offering pastilla,
low-priced snacks and excellent
set breakfasts with pancake-like
*msimmen*. For the rest of the
day, there are wonderful tajines
bubbling away out front to
tempt you. You can eat well
here for 60–80dh.

### CHEZ CHEGROUNI

Northeast corner of Pl Jemaa el Fna ☎0665
474615. Daily 8am–11pm.
MAP P.36–37, POCKET MAP B12

Popular with tourists, this place
does decent couscous and good
tajines at moderate prices
(mostly 60dh a throw, with
vegetarian options at 40dh),
though the portions are on the
small side. Come at a quiet
time if you want to bag one of
the seats on the upstairs terrace
overlooking the square.

### EARTH CAFÉ

1 Derb el Zouaq, off Rue Riad Zitoun el
Kedim ☎0661 289402, ✆earthcafemarrakech
.com. Daily 11am–10pm. MAP P.36–37, POCKET
MAP B13

Marrakesh's first vegetarian
restaurant offers nine dishes
(at 70–80dh a throw), of
which five are vegan. Choices
include veggie burgers,
"warm salad" and filo pastry
parcels containing various
combinations of vegetables
and sometimes cheese. The
portions are generous, and the
food is well prepared and
delicious, enough to tempt
any carnivore – all in all, it's a
nice change from the usual
Moroccan fare. They also
serve excellent juices and
herbal infusions, and the
atmosphere is intimate and
relaxed. The café has another
branch at 1 Derb Nakous, off
Rue Road Zitoun el Jadid.

### EL BAHJA

24 Rue Ben Marine ☎0524 441351. Daily
noon–11pm. MAP P.36–37, POCKET MAP B13

This place, whose patron has
appeared on a British TV food
programme, is popular with
locals and tourists alike. It's
good value, cheap and
generally unexciting, though its
kofta is highly rated and don't
miss the house yoghurt for
afters. Set menus 70–80dh.

### HADJ MUSTAPHA

Souk Ableuh ☎ 0661 344341. Daily 8am–9pm. MAP P.36–37, POCKET MAP B12
One of a trio of cheap hole-in-the-wall diners selling tanjia, the most quintessential of Marrakshi dishes (see box, p.42)– this is where working-class locals come to eat it. If you drop by in advance, you can have it cooked to order.

### HOTEL ISLANE TERRASSE PANORAMIQUE

279 Av Mohammed V ☎ 0524 440081. Daily 7am–10.30pm. MAP P.36–37, POCKET MAP A12
The main attraction at this rooftop restaurant is its unparalleled view of the Koutoubia rather than its not-very-good-value set menu (120dh). That said, its breakfast buffet (55dh) isn't bad.

### JNANE MOGADOR

Jnane Mogador Hotel, Derb Sidi Bouloukat ☎ 0524 426323. MAP P.36–37, POCKET MAP B12
Tuck into a tasty set menu (90–150dh) with couscous or tajine in the roof terrace restaurant of this little hotel, and round it off with a relaxing glass of fine mint tea. The service is every bit as good as in places charging twice the price, and it's a very handy bit of respite from the hustle and bustle on the streets below.

## Jemaa food stalls

Marrakesh's tourist guides often suggest that the Jemaa's food stalls (open daily from dusk until 11pm; MAP P.36–37, POCKET MAP B12) aren't very hygienic, and it's true that cases of food poisoning are not unknown. As well as couscous and pastilla, there are spicy **merguez sausages**, salads, fried fish and – for the more adventurous – **sheep's heads** complete with eyes.

To partake, sit on one of the benches and order. If you want a drink the stallholders will send a boy to get it for you. Note that stalls that don't clearly display their prices are likely to overcharge you mercilessly, so ask the price before ordering. If bread and olives are placed in front of you, you will be charged for them. You can avoid all this by just having a bowl of **harira** at one of the soup stalls.

Besides sit-down meals, you'll find exotic snacks on offer too. Over towards the eastern side of the square, a group of stalls offer a food much loved in Morocco – **stewed snails**. The stallholder ladles servings out of a simmering vat, and you eat the snails with a pin or toothpick before slurping back the soup they are stewed in. Just south of the main food stalls are a row of vendors selling **khoudenjal**, a hot, spicy infusion based on dried galangal and said to be an aphrodisiac. It's usually accompanied by a spicy confection made of flour and ground nuts, and served by the spoonful.

## Tajine and Tanjia

Morocco's most typical dish is the **tajine**, a term that correctly refers not to the food itself – vegetables piled up around a meat core – but rather to the vessel in which it is cooked, a heavy ceramic plate crowned with a conical ceramic lid in which the contents are cooked slowly over a low light, or over charcoal. The two classic tajines are chicken with olives and pickled lemon, and beef or lamb with prunes and almonds.

More specific to Marrakesh is the **tanjia** (also spelt tangia or tanzhiya), a jug in which beef or lamb are stewed even more slowly. The traditional way to cook a tanjia is in the embers of a bathhouse furnace, and indeed if you order in advance at diners such as *Hadj Mustapha* (see p.41), the meat and seasonings (garlic, cumin, nutmeg and other spices) will be placed in the urn for you and taken to the man who stokes the furnace at the local hammam. When the urn emerges from the embers a few hours later, the meat is tender and ready to eat.

### KASSABINE CAFÉ

77 Rue Dabbachi, by Kissariat Quessabine ⓣ 0665 293796. Daily 9am–11pm. MAP P.37

The sunny terrace of this bright little café-restaurant has a perfect vista over the busy street below and views all the way down the western branch of the Jemaa el Fna. The tajines are lovingly made and include a wonderful beef with courgettes as well as old favourites like beef with prunes and almonds or chicken with lemon and olive, all for around 50dh.

LE TOBSIL

### LE MARRAKCHI

52 Rue des Banques ⓣ 0524 443377, ⓦ lemarrakchi.com. Daily noon–3pm & 7pm–midnight. MAP P.36–37, POCKET MAP B12

High up above the square, *Le Marrakchi* has imperial but intimate decor and impeccable service. The food, too, is superb, and includes delicious pastilla, and several couscous and tajine options, including vegetarian. Main dishes are mostly around 130–180dh. Licensed.

### LE TOBSIL

22 Derb Moulay Abdallah Ben Hezzaien ⓣ 0524 444052. Daily except Tues 7.30–11pm. MAP P.36–37, POCKET MAP A12

The Moroccan cuisine is sumptuous at this intimate riad, which is considered by many to be the finest restaurant in town. It's reached by heading south down a little alley just east of Bab Laksour. Highlights include a delicious pastilla and the most aromatic couscous you could imagine, though the wine (included in the price) doesn't match the food in quality. The set menu – which changes daily – is 640dh. Worth booking ahead.

## LES PRÉMICES

Pl Jemaa el Fna ☎ 0524 391970. Daily
8–11.30pm. MAP P.36–37, POCKET MAP B12
*Les Prémices* serves decent
Moroccan and European food,
including tasty gazpacho,
good-value tajines, steaks, fish,
pizzas and even crème brûlée.
It's on the very southeastern
corner of the square, but close
enough for a view of the action,
and very moderately priced
(you can eat well for 120dh,
very well for 160dh).

## PIZZERIA PORTOFINO

279 Av Mohammed V ☎ 0524 391665. Daily
noon–midnight. MAP P.36–37, POCKET MAP A12
The wood-oven pizzas
(55–70dh) here are well cooked,
if slightly bland, and the
ambience is quite posh, with
white tablecloths and uniformed
waiters. They also have pasta
(70–90dh) and a "Marrakshi"
lamb risotto (80dh).

## RESTAURANT ARGANA

North side of Pl Jemaa el Fna.
MAP P.36–37, POCKET MAP B12
*Argana* is the closest vantage
point to the action in the
square, making it extremely
popular with tourists.
Unfortunately this also made it
the target of a 2011 bomb
attack, which killed sixteen
people, but it is expected to
reopen during 2015.

## RESTAURANT OSCAR PROGRÈS

20 Rue Ben Marine ☎ 0666 937147. Daily
noon–11pm. MAP P.36–37, POCKET MAP B13
One of the best budget
restaurants in town, with
friendly service and large
servings of couscous (go for
that or the brochettes in
preference to the tajines, which
are rather bland). You can fill
up here for around 65dh, or be
a real pig and choose the 100dh
set menu.

LES PRÉMICES

THE JEMAA EL FNA AND THE KOUTOUBIA

## TAJ'IN DARNA

50 Pl Jemaa el Fna ☎ 0670 213191,
🌐 tajindarna.com. Daily 7am–11pm.
MAP P.36–37, POCKET MAP B12
In great location on the
northeastern arm of the Jemaa,
you can dine on a variety of
tajines, from chicken with
lemon and olive (40dh) to less
familiar varieties such as rabbit
"grandmother style" (with
vegetables and raisins; 70dh).
Some dishes cost slightly more
if taken on the scenic terrace.

# Bar

## GRAND HOTEL TAZI

Corner of Rue Bab Agnaou and Rue el
Mouahidine ☎ 0524 442787. Daily 24hr.
MAP P.36–37, POCKET MAP B13
This was once the only place in
the Medina where you could
get a drink, and it's still the
cheapest (beers from 25dh).
There's nothing fancy about the
bar area – squeezed in between
the restaurant and the lobby,
and frequently spilling over
into the latter – but it manages
to be neither rough nor
pretentious, a rare feat among
Marrakesh drinking dens.

# The Northern Medina

Just north of the Jemaa el Fna begins the bustling main souk – or market – area, which is focused on a central thoroughfare, Souk Smarine, and is great for souvenir shopping. Originally, each souk was clearly defined, with one street selling this and another selling that, though these distinctions have now blurred somewhat. Among the most interesting souks are the Rahba Kedima, with its quirky apothecary stalls, and the dyers' souk, hung with brightly coloured hanks of freshly dyed wool. North of the souks are the small but architecturally important Almoravid Koubba, the Marrakesh Museum and the beautifully decorated Ben Youssef Medersa. Beyond, in all directions, stretches a vast residential area with more workaday shops and few tourists. The area is not devoid of attractions, however, containing a couple of important religious shrines and the city's stinky but fascinating tanneries.

## SOUK SMARINE

MAP P.46–47, POCKET MAP B11

Busy and crowded, Souk Smarine, the souks' main thoroughfare, is covered along its whole course by an iron trellis with slats across it that restricts the sun to **shafts of**

SOUK SMARINE

**light** dappling everything beneath, especially in the early afternoon. Historically the street was dominated by the sale of textiles and clothing. Today, classier tourist "bazaars" are moving in, with American Express signs in the windows, but there are still dozens of shops in the arcades selling and tailoring traditional shirts and kaftans. Other shops specialize in multicoloured cotton skullcaps and in **fezzes** (*tarbouche fassi* in Arabic), which originate from the city of Fez in northern Morocco. The feeling of being in a labyrinth of hidden treasures is heightened by the **passages** in between the shops, many of which lead through to small covered markets. The occasional stucco-covered doorways between shops are entrances to mosques – havens of spiritual refreshment amid the bustle.

## RAHBA KEDIMA

MAP P.46–47, POCKET MAP B11–C13

Souk Smarine narrows just before the fork at its northern end. The passageways to the right (east) here lead through to Rahba Kedima, an open marketplace with stalls in the middle and around the outside.

Immediately to the right as you go in is **Souk Loghzal**, once a market for slaves, more recently for wool, but now mainly selling secondhand clothes. In Rahba Kedima itself, the most interesting stalls are those belonging to the **apothecaries** in the southwest corner of the square, selling **traditional cosmetics** – earthenware saucers of cochineal (*kashiniah*) for lip-rouge, powdered kohl eyeliner (usually lead sulphide, which is toxic), henna (the only cosmetic unmarried Moroccan women are supposed to use) and sticks of *suek* (walnut root or bark) for cleaning teeth. The same stalls also sell herbal and animal ingredients still in widespread use for spells and medicinal cures. As well as aphrodisiac roots and tablets, you'll see dried pieces of lizard and stork, fragments of beaks, talons and other bizarre animal products. Some shops (to be avoided) also sell gazelle skulls, leopard skins and other products from illegally poached endangered wild animals. The *Café des Épices* (see p.56) overlooks the square and is a good place to take a breather.

## LA CRIÉE BERBÈRE

Souk des Tapis. MAP P.46–47, POCKET MAP C11

Until the French occupied the city in 1912, La Criée Berbère (the Berber auction) was the site of **slave auctions**, held just before sunset every Wednesday, Thursday and Friday. Most of

RAHBA KEDIMA

the slaves had been kidnapped and marched here with the camel caravans from West Africa – those too weak to make it were left to die en route. Happily, only rugs and carpets are sold here nowadays.

## KISSARIA

MAP P.46–47, POCKET MAP B10

A covered market at the heart of the souks, the Kissaria was originally set up as the souk for rich imported **fabrics**. It remains the centre for cloth and clothing, with an array of beautiful dresses, flowing headscarves and roll upon roll of fine material on show.

## SOUK SABBAGHINE

MAP P.46–47, POCKET MAP B10

The Souk Sabbaghine (or Souk des Teinturiers, the **dyers' souk**) is west of the Kissaria and very near the sixteenth-century Mouassine Mosque and fountain. On a good day, it has a splendid array of freshly dyed sheaves of wool in a multitude of colours hung out to dry. At other times you'll barely see any at all, though you can still take a look as the dyers boil up their tints and prepare the wool for treatment.

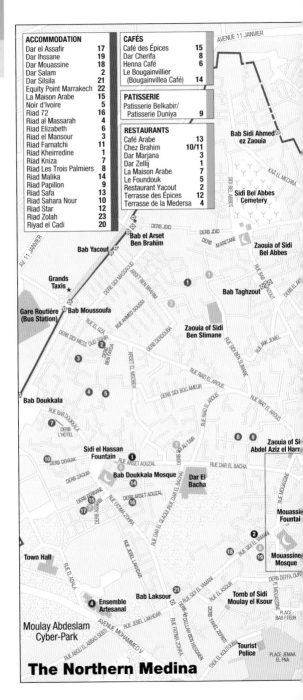

| ACCOMMODATION | |
|---|---|
| Dar el Assafir | 17 |
| Dar Ihssane | 19 |
| Dar Mouassine | 18 |
| Dar Salam | 2 |
| Dar Silsila | 21 |
| Equity Point Marrakech | 22 |
| La Maison Arabe | 15 |
| Noir d'Ivoire | 5 |
| Riad 72 | 16 |
| Riad al Massarah | 4 |
| Riad Elizabeth | 6 |
| Riad el Mansour | 3 |
| Riad Farnatchi | 11 |
| Riad Kheirredine | 1 |
| Riad Kniza | 7 |
| Riad Les Trois Palmiers | 8 |
| Riad Malika | 14 |
| Riad Papillon | 9 |
| Riad Safa | 13 |
| Riad Sahara Nour | 10 |
| Riad Star | 12 |
| Riad Zolah | 23 |
| Riyad el Cadi | 20 |

| CAFÉS | |
|---|---|
| Café des Épices | 15 |
| Dar Cherifa | 8 |
| Henna Café | 6 |
| Le Bougainvillier | |
| (Bougainvillea Café) | 14 |

| PATISSERIE | |
|---|---|
| Patisserie Belkabir/ | |
| Patisserie Duniya | 9 |

| RESTAURANTS | |
|---|---|
| Café Arabe | 13 |
| Chez Brahim | 10/11 |
| Dar Marjana | 3 |
| Dar Zellij | 1 |
| La Maison Arabe | 7 |
| Le Foundouk | 5 |
| Restaurant Yacout | 2 |
| Terrasse des Épices | 12 |
| Terrasse de la Medersa | 4 |

# The Northern Medina

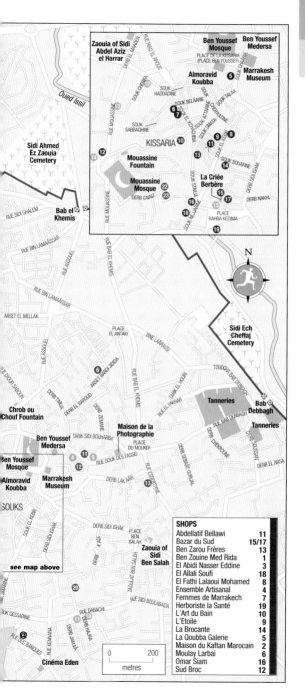

## SOUK HADDADINE AND SOUK CHERRATINE

MAP P.46-47, POCKET MAP B18 & C18

It's easy to locate Souk Haddadine, the **ironmongers' souk**, by ear – just head towards the source of the bangings and clangings as the artisans shape raw metal into decorative window grilles, lampstands and furniture. Close at hand you'll find Souk Cherratine, the **leather-workers' souk**, full of workshops where hats, slippers and other goods are cut and stitched by hand. There are also specialist shops whose sole occupation is to grind and sharpen tools.

## MARRAKESH MUSEUM

Pl de la Kissaria (Pl Ben Youssef) Ⓦ museedemarrakech.ma. Daily 9am-6pm. 50dh. MAP P.46-47, POCKET MAP C18

This magnificent late nineteenth-century palace, originally built for Morocco's defence minister, is now a museum housing exhibitions of Moroccan **art and sculpture**. It's the building itself, however, that's most memorable, especially the warren of rooms that was once the **hammam**,

and the now-covered **inner courtyard** with its huge brass lamp hung above a central fountain.

## ALMORAVID KOUBBA

South side of Pl de la Kissaria (Pl Ben Youssef). Daily 9am-6pm, but closed for restoration at time of writing. MAP P.46-47, POCKET MAP C18

Situated well below the current ground level, the Almoravid Koubba (correctly called the Koubba Ba'adyin) doesn't look like much, but this small, two-storey structure is the only building in Morocco to survive intact from the eleventh-century Almoravid dynasty, whose style lies at the root of all Moroccan architecture. The windows on each side exhibit the classic shapes of Moroccan design – as do the merlons (the Christmas-tree-like battle-ments). Its motifs – notably pine cones, palms and acanthus leaves – appear again in later buildings such as the nearby Ben Youssef Medersa. The Almoravid Koubba was probably an ablutions annexe to the **Ben Youssef Mosque** opposite, which, like almost all the Almoravids' buildings, was demolished and rebuilt by the succeeding Almohad dynasty. The *koubba* is currently closed, supposedly for restoration, but can be seen very well from Place de la Kissaria.

## BEN YOUSSEF MEDERSA

Off Pl de la Kissaria (Pl Ben Youssef). Daily 9am-5pm. 60dh. MAP P.46-47, POCKET MAP C18

Just north of the Marrakesh Museum, and attached to the Ben Youssef Mosque, is the Ben Youssef Medersa, a **religious school** where students learned the Koran by rote. The medersa was founded in the fourteenth century and almost completely rebuilt in the 1560s under the

ALMORAVID KOUBBA

BEN YOUSSEF MEDERSA

Saadian dynasty. The central courtyard, its carved **cedar lintels** weathered almost flat on the most exposed side, is unusually large. Along two sides run wide, sturdy, columned arcades, and above them are some of the windows of the dormitory quarters, which are reached by stairs from the entry vestibule. The decoration is at its best preserved and most elaborate in the **prayer hall**, at the far end of the main court. Notable here, as in the courtyard's cedar carving, is a predominance of pine cone and palm motifs, especially around the horseshoe-arched mihrab. The inscriptions are quotations from the Koran, the most common being its opening invocation: "In the name of God, the Compassionate, the Merciful".

## Fondouks

One of the most characteristic types of building in the Medina is the **fondouk** or caravanserai, originally inns used by visiting merchants when they were in Marrakesh to trade in its souks. *Fondouks* have a courtyard in the middle surrounded by what were originally stables, while the upper level contained rooms for the merchants. Some *fondouks* date back to Saadian times (1520–1669).

Today, Marrakesh's *fondouks* are in varying states of repair; some have become private residences, others commercial premises. Some have been converted to house tourist souvenir shops, and welcome visitors, but even in others, the doors to the courtyards are often left open, and no one seems to mind if you wander in to have a look.

Interesting *fondouks* include: a group on Rue Dar el Bacha by the junction with Rue Mouassine, several of which welcome visitors; a couple just south of the junction on Rue Mouassine itself; a row on the south side of Rue Bab Debbagh, behind the Ben Youssef Medersa; a whole series along Rue Amesfah, north of the Ben Youssef Mosque; and one directly opposite the Chrob ou Chouf fountain. And of course there's **Le Foundouk** (see p.59) and **Terrasse le Medersa** (see p.59), where you can eat in a converted *fondouk*.

# The Seven Saints of Marrakesh

Some two hundred holy men and women, known as **marabouts**, are buried in Marrakesh. A *marabout's* tomb can become the centrepiece of a mosque-mausoleum called a **zaouia**, often the focus for a brotherhood of the *marabout's* followers, who usually belong to the mystic branch of Islam known as **Sufism**. It's widely believed that praying to God at the tomb of a *marabout* attracts a special *beraka* (blessing).

Marrakesh's seven most prominent *marabouts* are usually referred to in English as the "Seven Saints" of the city, though they have little in common aside from being buried here. The most prominent, Sidi Bel Abbes, has become pretty much the city's patron saint.

Though non-Muslims are not allowed to enter the tombs, you can certainly see them all from the outside, and a couple – **Sidi Bel Abbes** (p.52) and **Sidi Abdel Aziz el Harrar** (see below) – are definitely worth a look.

## CHROB OU CHOUF FOUNTAIN

220 Rue Assouel, a little way north of Pl de la Kissaria (Pl Ben Youssef). MAP P.46–47, POCKET MAP G4

This small sixteenth-century recessed fountain (its name means "drink and admire") is mainly notable for its carved cedar lintel, which incorporates calligraphy and stalactite-like projections. Back in the days before people had running water at home, paying to put up a fountain was a pious act of charity, sanctioned by the Koran. Religious institutions and wealthy philanthropists had them installed to provide not only drinking water, but also a place to wash – most notably to perform the ritual ablutions demanded by the Koran before prayer, which is why so many of the surviving fountains are attached to mosques.

## ZAOUIA OF SIDI ABDEL AZIZ EL HARRAR

Rue Mouassine. MAP P.46–47, POCKET MAP B10

Sidi Abdel Aziz el Harrar (d.1508) was an Islamic scholar who – unusually among Marrakesh's Seven Saints (see box above) – was actually born in Marrakesh, though he made his name in Fez. His *zaouia* is one of the smallest of the Seven Saints' shrines, but like the others it has a distinctive red-and-yellow pattern around the top, just below the roof, indicating that it is part of the pilgrimage circuit established here in the seventeenth century.

## BAB DOUKKALA MOSQUE

Rue Bab Doukkala. MAP P.46–47, POCKET MAP F4

Serving the lively Bab Doukkala quarter, this *pisé* mosque with its elegant brick minaret was constructed in 1557–58 on the orders of Lalla Messaouda,

CHROB OU CHOUF FOUNTAIN

mother of Ahmed el Mansour, the most illustrious sultan of the Saadian dynasty. On the main street in front of the mosque is the impressive three-bay **Sidi el Hassan fountain**, now converted into a small art gallery (which is sometimes open for exhibitions).

## ZAOUIA OF SIDI BEN SALAH

Pl Ben Salah. MAP P.46–47, POCKET MAP H5

This fourteenth-century holy man's tomb is one of the few important buildings in the Medina to have been put up under the Merenid dynasty, who had moved the Moroccan capital from Marrakesh to its rival city of Fez. The most prominent feature is the handsome **minaret**, covered with brilliant green tiles in a *darj w ktarf* pattern. The square in front of the *zaouia* is usually pretty lively with fruit and vegetable sellers and other traders, and gives a flavour of Medina life away from tourism.

## THE TANNERIES

Along and off Rue Bab Debbagh. MAP P.46–47, POCKET MAP J4

Marrakesh's tanneries are sited at the edge of the city not only because of the smell, but also for access to water: a stream, the Oued Issil, runs just outside the walls.

One tannery that's easy to find is Tannerie Attanjir on the north side of the street about 200m before Bab Debbagh, opposite the blue-tiled fountain, with another one about 200m further west. If you want to take a closer look at the **tanning process**, come in the morning, when the cooperatives are at work. There is no charge to visit the tanneries – ignore hustlers who tell you otherwise.

## MAISON DE LA PHOTOGRAPHIE

46 Rue Souk des Fassis ☎ 0524 385 721, ⓦ maisondelaphotographie.ma. Daily 9.30am–7pm. 40dh. MAP P.46–47, POCKET MAP H4

The Maison de la Photographie houses a reasonably interesting collection of early twentieth-century (and a few late nineteenth-century) photographs of Morocco, some made from glass negatives. The photographs are exhibited over three floors, with one room dedicated to pictures of the Jemaa el Fna, and the terrace gives good views over the Medina rooftops.

## BAB DEBBAGH

MAP P.46–47, POCKET MAP J4

Among the more interesting of Marrakesh's city gates, Bab Debbagh is supposedly Almoravid in design. Over the years it must have been almost totally rebuilt, but its defensive purpose is still apparent: three internal **chicanes** are placed in such a manner as to force anyone attempting to storm it to make numerous turns. Just before the gate, several shops on the left give good **views** over the tanneries from their roofs. Shopkeepers may invite you up, but agree the price first or you'll be mercilessly overcharged.

## BAB EL KHEMIS

MAP P.46–47, POCKET MAP H2

This beautiful gate, originally Almoravid though rebuilt under the Almohads, is surrounded by concentric rings of decoration and topped with Christmas-tree-like castellations. Its name, meaning "Thursday Gate", is a reference to the market held outside, 300m to the north. You'll find stalls out most days, but the main market is on Thursday mornings. It mainly sells local produce, though the odd handicraft item does occasionally surface.

## ZAOUIA OF SIDI BEL ABBES

Rue Bab Taghzout. MAP P.46–47, POCKET MAP G3

The most important of Marrakesh's Seven Saints, twelfth-century **Sidi Bel Abbes** was a prolific performer of miracles, particularly famed for giving sight to the blind. The huge mosque that now houses his tomb, with a green-tiled roof and surrounding outbuildings, dates largely from an early eighteenth-century reconstruction. It lies just north of **Bab Taghzout**, which was one of the gates of the Medina until the eighteenth century, when Sultan Mohammed Abdallah extended the walls north to include the Sidi Bel Abbes quarter. As with all *zaouias*, non-Muslims are not allowed to enter the complex but may take a look in from the outside. The foundation that runs the *zaouia* also owns much of the surrounding quarter and is engaged in charitable work, distributing food each evening to the blind.

BAB EL KHEMIS

# Shops

### ABDELLATIF BELLAWI

56 & 103 Kissariat Lossta, between Souk el Kebir and Souk Attarine ☎ 0668 049114. Daily except Fri 9am–5pm. MAP P.46–47, POCKET MAP B10

This pair of costume-jewellery and knick-knack shops has a great selection of beads and bangles, including Berber bracelets from the Atlas in chunky solid silver, traditional Berber necklaces, West African money beads and necklaces from as far away as Yemen. There are more frivolous items too, like the cowrie-encrusted Gnaoua caps hanging up outside the door, plus rings, earrings and woollen Berber belts.

### BAZAR DU SUD

14 & 117 Souk des Tapis ☎ 0524 443004. Daily 9am–7pm. MAP P.46–47, POCKET MAP C11

There are carpets here from all over the south of Morocco. Most are claimed to be old (if you prefer them spanking new, pop next door to Bazar Jouti at nos. 16 & 119), and most are coloured with wonderful natural dyes such as saffron (yellow), cochineal (red) and indigo (blue). A large carpet could cost 5000dh or more, but you might be able to find a small rug for around 500dh.

### BEN ZOUINE MED RIDA

142 Rue Arset Aouzal ☎ 0524 385056. Sat–Thurs 8am–8pm, Fri 8am–noon. MAP P.46–47, POCKET MAP F4

For a tailor-made local-style shirt or blouse, be it in cotton, linen or wool, this is the place to come, though opening hours can be a bit haphazard (morning is the best time to catch them). You just choose your cloth, get measured up,

ABDELLATIF BELLAWI

specify what buttons or even embroidered design you want, and come back a day or two later to collect. Expect to pay around 400–1000dh.

### BENZARROU JAÂFAR

1 Kissariat Drouj, off Souk Smata by no. 116 ☎ 0524 443351. Daily 8am–7.30pm. MAP P.46–47, POCKET MAP B11

There are any number of shops in this souk selling Moroccan slippers, or *babouches*, but while emporiums in the Souk des Babouches specialize in new designs, this trio of shops in a little corner of the Kissaria is the best place to come for the traditional variety. Both men's and women's are available, in various colours. Prices start at 50dh, and there's no pressure or hard sell.

### EL ABIDI NASSER EDDINE

9 Souk Smarine ☎ 0524 427668. Daily 9am–9pm. MAP P.46–47, POCKET MAP B11

A discreet and rather upmarket shop for antique jewellery, or modern designer pieces, all exquisite, all expensive, plus silverware, manuscripts and some very fine *objets d'art*. A place for those seeking something finer than the usual souk wares.

## EL ALLALI SOUFI

125 Souk Nejjarine, opposite the alley to Pl Rahba Kedima ☏ 0668 440399. Daily 9am–8pm. MAP P.46–47, POCKET MAP B11

This little place sells silver – old and new – whether in the form of jewellery, old coins, spoons and ladles, teapots, or just odd little curiosities (some in other metals, such as brass). Pricey, but worth a browse.

## EL FATHI LALAOUI MOHAMED

8 Souk Serrajine, off Souk el Kebir. Daily except Fri 9am–7pm. ☏ 0668 964629. MAP P.46–47, POCKET MAP C10

This shop originally sold saddles for horses (and the one next door still does), but now specializes in selling objects made from the layer of woollen felt that formed part of the traditional saddle – turned into bags, hats, even beads. Each item is made in a single piece with a big splash of colour. Bags go for 150–250dh, hats for 100dh.

## ENSEMBLE ARTISANAL

Av Mohammed V, midway between the Koutoubia and Bab Nkob ☏ 0524 443503. Mon–Sat 9am–7pm, Sun 9am–noon. MAP P.46–47, POCKET MAP E5

This government-run complex of small arts and crafts shops

ENSEMBLE ARTISANAL

holds a reasonable range of goods, notably leather, textiles and carpets. The prices, which are more or less fixed, are a good gauge of the going rate if you intend to bargain elsewhere. At the back are a dozen or so workshops where you can watch young people learning a range of crafts.

## FEMMES DE MARRAKECH

67 Souk el Kchachbia, west of the Almoravid Koubba ☏ 0665 343472. Daily except Fri 10am–6pm (later in summer). MAP P.46–47, POCKET MAP B10

A dress shop run by a women's cooperative, who create their own garments and also sell – on a fair-trade basis – clothes made at home by other women. The dresses are handmade from pure cotton and linen fabrics in a mix of Moroccan and Western styles, with colours ranging from sober pinks and greys to bright orange tie-dye.

## HERBORISTE LA SANTÉ

152 Pl Rahba Kedima, on the south side of the square ☏ 0666 310728. Daily 8.30am–7pm. MAP P.46–47, POCKET MAP C11

One of a row of apothecary shops on the south and west side of the Rahba Kedima, but unlike some others, this one doesn't sell dubious animal products. The genial staff will patiently explain the wondrous properties of the various herbs, spices, scents and traditional cosmetics they sell.

## L'ART DU BAIN

13 Souk el Labadine ☏ 0668 445942. Daily 9am–7pm. MAP P.46–47, POCKET MAP B10

This place sells a big range of soaps made with real essential oils, mostly Moroccan. The range of scents includes old favourites such as lavender, and more unusual ones such as cinnamon, all available in small (30dh) or large (40dh).

## MAISON DU CAFTAN MAROCAIN

65 Rue Sidi el Yamani ☎ 0524 441051. Daily 10.30am–8pm. MAP P.46–47, POCKET MAP B11

All sorts of robes, tunics and kaftans are available in this wonderful shop, from see-through glittery gowns and sequinned velvet tunics to lush embroidered silk kaftans that make sumptuous housecoats (albeit mostly at prices in excess of 2000dh). Most are for women, but there are also a few men's garments. Past customers include Jean-Paul Gaultier and Mick Jagger.

## MOULAY LARBAI

96 Souk el Kchachbia. ☎ 0671 374042. Sat–Thurs 8am–7pm, Fri 8am–noon & 5–7pm. MAP P.46–47, POCKET MAP B10

Moulay Larbai's claim to fame is that it was he who first started making mirrors framed with small pieces of mirror or of coloured glass. He still makes the best ones in the souk, with proper Iraqi-style stained glass for the colours, and they come in various shapes and sizes. Prices start at around 50dh.

## LA BROCANTE

16 Souk Souafine, off Souk el Kebir. Daily except Mon 10am–1pm & 3–6.30pm. MAP P.46–47, POCKET MAP C11

A little shop with all sorts of antique curiosities: corkscrews, toys, watches, medals, enamelled metal signs and what would be just bric-a-brac, but for the fact that it's clearly been chosen with a tasteful eye.

## LA QOUBBA GALERIE

91 Souk Talaa ☎ 0524 390371. Daily 9am–4pm. MAP P.46–47, POCKET MAP C10

Paintings and sculptures by contemporary Marrakshi artists are displayed in an attractive little two-room gallery off Place de la Kissaria (Pl Ben Youssef). The *qoubba* (dome) after which it's named surmounts the building behind.

## L'ÉTOILE

13 Souk el Kebir. Daily 10am–7pm. MAP P.47

This unobtrusive little shop does a nifty line in goods recycled from flour sacks, which include, as you might expect, handbags (don't worry: they're waterproofed) and purses (ditto), but also *babouches* (slippers) and even lampshades.

## OMAR SIAM

39 Souk Nejjarine, part of Souk el Kebir. ☎ 0641 21171. Daily, no fixed hours but usually noon–8pm, and some mornings. MAP P.46–47, POCKET MAP B11

It's not much more than a hole in the wall, but stop for a peek at Omar Siam's range of wooden spoons, handmade in all sizes, and really quite charming in their own small way. There are ladles for eating *harira*, smaller ones for measuring spices, spoons that you could stir your tea with, spoons with holes for fishing olives out of brine, and non-spoon items too: pastry moulds for making Moroccan sweets, and even pairs of wooden scissors (for cutting fresh pasta, in case you wondered). Prices are fixed and the smallest items are just 10dh.

## SUD BROC

65 Rue Mouassine ☎ 0666 075155. Mon–Thurs, Sat & Sun 9am–8.30 pm except Fri 3–8.30pm. MAP P.46–47, POCKET MAP B11

A bric-a-brac shop, not as good as *La Brocante* (see p.54) and with quite high prices (bargain hard), but it does have an interesting selection, including old cameras, watches, lighters – Zippos and imitation Zippos, old and new – and other relics of the good old days.

# Cafés

## CAFÉ DES ÉPICES

73 Pl Rahba Kedima ☎ 0524 391770, ⓦ cafedesepices.net. Daily 9.30am–9pm. MAP P.46–47, POCKET MAP C11

Café offering refuge from the hubbub and views over the Rahba Kedima from the upper floor and the roof terrace. Drinks include orange juice, mint tea, coffee in various permutations, including spiced with cinnamon, and there are also sandwiches (40–50dh) and salads (50–55dh).

## DAR CHERIFA

8 Derb Charfa Lakbir, Mouassine ☎ 0524 426463, ⓦ darcherifa.com. Daily 10am–8pm (ring for entry). MAP P.46–47, POCKET MAP B11

For those who like a bit of culture with their tea and pastry, riad rental firm Marrakech Riads (see box, p.105) run an art-house literary café at their HQ. It's a lovely fifteenth-century riad, complete with antique doors, stucco and carved cedar, where you can stop for a spot of tea, a light lunch or even couscous (the best in the Medina, so they reckon). As well as food and refreshment, the café offers art exhibitions, cultural evenings, poetry readings (in Arabic, Berber and French) and even concerts.

## HENNA CAFÉ

93 Rue Arset Aouzal ☎ 0656 566374, ⓦ hennacafemarrakech.com. Daily 11am–8pm. MAP P.46–47, POCKET MAP F4

As well as tea and coffee, this café offers salads and snacks that are slightly different from the Marrakesh norm (falafel and tahina, for example, at 40dh),

DAR CHERIFA

LE BOUGAINVILLIER

and there's a terrace on the roof as well as the downstairs café. They also have a henna menu, where you can choose a henna tattoo (50–550dh), and all profits are ploughed back into the local community.

### LE BOUGAINVILLIER (BOUGAINVILLEA CAFÉ)

33 Rue Mouassine ☎ 0618 378067. Daily 10am–10pm. MAP P.46–47, POCKET MAP B11
An upmarket café and quiet retreat in the middle of the Medina: handy for a break after a hard morning's shopping in the souks. Set in a secluded patio, it tries hard to be stylish, and generally succeeds, the lack of actual bougainvillea flowers being made up for by bougainvillea-pink paintwork and chairs. There are salads, sandwiches, cakes, juices, coffee and tea, but most of all it's a pleasant space in which to relax.

# Patisserie

### PATISSERIE BELKABIR / PATISSERIE DUNIYA

63–65 Souk Smarine, by the corner of Traverse el Ksour. Daily 10am–9pm. MAP P.46–47, POCKET MAP B11

Side by side, these shops specialize in traditional Moroccan sweetmeats, stuffed with nuts and drenched in syrup, which are particularly popular during the holy month of Ramadan (when of course they are eaten by night). A mixture (*mélange*) is 100dh a kilo – this price is posted up, but beware of them trying to charge a higher rate.

# Restaurants

### CAFÉ ARABE

184 Rue Mouassine ☎ 0524 429728. Daily 10am–11pm (food served from noon). MAP P.46–47, POCKET MAP B10
A sophisticated bar and restaurant in the heart of the Medina and very handy for the souks. As well as excellent Moroccan and European cooking, not to mention snappy service, there's a fine selection of alcoholic drinks including wines and cocktails, plus juices, teas and mocktails, served on the terrace, in the patio or in the salon. Expect to pay around 300dh plus drinks.

### CHEZ BRAHIM

38 & 86 Rue Dabbachi ☎ 0524 024709. Daily noon–11pm. MAP P.46–47, POCKET MAP C11 & C12
These two budget restaurants 100m apart each offer rooftop dining with the usual range of Moroccan staples (salads, brochettes, tajines, couscous), and set menus (60–120dh), the cheapest of which change daily and differs slightly between the two branches. *Chez Brahim* #1, at no. 38, has music in the evenings, when the *menu* costs 20–30dh more, while *Chez Brahim* #2 has a patisserie downstairs and slightly less kitsch decor upstairs, but both are good value and try hard to please.

## DAR MARJANA

15 Derb Sidi Ali Tair, off Rue Arset Aouzal
☎ 0524 385110, ⓦ darmarjanamarrakech
.com. Daily except Tues from 8pm. Advance
booking only. MAP P.46–47, POCKET MAP A10

This restaurant is housed in a
beautiful early nineteenth-
century palace. Look for the
sign above the entrance to a
passageway diagonally across
the street from the corner of the
Dar el Glaoui; take the passage
and look for the green door
facing you before a right turn.
Among the tasty dishes they
serve, two classics stand out:
poultry pastilla and *couscous
aux sept légumes*. The set menu
costs 726dh including wine.

## DAR YACOUT

79 Derb Sidi Ahmed Soussi ☎ 0524 382929,
ⓦ daryacout.com. Tues–Sun 8pm–midnight.
MAP P.46–47, POCKET MAP F3

Housed in a gorgeous old
palace, the *Yacout* opened as a
restaurant in 1987, its columns
and fireplaces made over in
super-smooth orange- and
blue-striped *tadelakt* plaster,
courtesy of American interior
designer and Marrakesh
resident Bill Willis. The owner
was formerly Marrakesh's
British consul. After a drink on

DAR MARJANA

the roof terrace, you move
down into one of the intimate
salons surrounding the
courtyard for a selection of
salads, followed by a tajine,
then lamb couscous and dessert
(the menu costs 700dh per
person including wine). The
classic Moroccan tajine of
chicken with lemon and olives
is a favourite here, but the fish
version is also highly rated. The
cuisine has in the past received
Michelin plaudits, though
standards are beginning to slip
as the tour groups move in.
Booking ahead is advised. The
easiest way to get there is by
*petit taxi* – the driver will
usually walk you to the door.

## DAR ZELLIJ

1 Kaa Essour, Sidi Ben Slimane ☎ 0524
382627, ⓦ darzellij.com. Daily except Tues
7pm–midnight, Fri & Sat noon–3pm & Sun
10am–3pm. MAP P.46–47, POCKET MAP F3

A seventeenth-century riad
where you can take dinner on
the patio or in one of the
lounges, all decked out in red
and super-comfortable. Start
with Moroccan salad and
*briouats* (filo pastry parcels –
the Moroccan equivalent of a
spring roll), followed by pastilla
and then a tajine (vegetarian
options are available), and
round it off with sweet pastilla
or orange in cinnamon. There's
a choice of set menus at
350–600dh, plus lunch (Fri–
Sun) at 200–250dh, not
including drinks. Also, there's
Sunday brunch at 180dh.
Licensed.

## LA MAISON ARABE

1 Derb Assehbi, Rue Bab Doukkala ☎ 0524
387010, ⓦ lamaisonarabe.com. Daily noon–3pm
& 7–11pm. MAP P.46–47, POCKET MAP E4

As well as being the city's best
hotel (see p.108), *La Maison
Arabe* is also one of its top
eating places, with two

DAR YACOUT

This terrace restaurant, above the souks, is run by the same people as *Café des Épices* (see p.56). It's well designed, with separate bays for each table giving diners their own space and a bit of privacy – handy if you want to use the free wi-fi – while still allowing you to enjoy the great views. Food is good and very moderately priced, with main dishes in the 95–140dh range. There's pastilla or a trio of Moroccan salads to start, and perhaps monkfish tajine to follow and crème brûlée and chocolate mousse. There's also a 120dh set menu.

restaurants, of which the Moroccan one serves up a 1000dh tasting menu for two including seasonal tajines and pastilla (or a veg pastilla and veg tajine for non-carnivores). The *Trois Saveurs* restaurant offers Moroccan, European and Asian dishes at around 200–250dh a go. Licensed.

## LE FOUNDOUK

55 Rue Souk des Fassis ☎ 0524 378190, ⓦ foundouk.com. Tues–Sun noon–midnight. MAP P.46–47, POCKET MAP C10

Housed in a beautifully converted former *fondouk*, this restaurant is conveniently located on the way from Ben Youssef Medersa to the tanneries. The menu has both Moroccan and international dishes, including tajines, *briouats* and brochettes, as well as more adventurous dishes such as a monkfish tajine, Thai-style chicken or breast of duck with caramelized endive. Main dishes go for 110–180dh. Licensed.

## TERRASSE DES ÉPICES

15 Souk Cherifa ☎ 0524 375904, ⓦ terrassedesepices.com. Daily 11am–11pm. MAP P.46–47, POCKET MAP B10

## TERRASSE LE MEDERSA

Fondouk Lahbabi, 4 Rue de Souk des Fassis ☎ 0524 390719. Daily 10am–10pm. MAP P.46–47, POCKET MAP C10

On the terrace of a *fondouk* adjoining the roof of the Ben Youssef Medersa (hence its name), this unassuming little café-restaurant offers a variety of mocktails (35–40dh), juices and inexpensive Moroccan dishes (chicken tajine with lemon and olive, for example, at 55dh), served with a smile. On the downside, the seats could be larger and more comfortable.

TERRASSE DES ÉPICES

# The Southern Medina and Agdal Gardens

The southern part of the Medina is less crowded and frenetic than the northern part, and is broken up into more distinct quarters. Its biggest attractions are the fabulous ruin of the El Badi Palace and the exquisite Saadian Tombs. Both lie within the Kasbah district, which was originally Marrakesh's walled citadel. To the east of here, and occupying a substantial area, is the Royal Palace, used by the king when visiting the city (and not open to the public). The area further east of this is the Mellah, once Morocco's largest Jewish ghetto; the extensive Agdal Gardens lie to the south. Between the Royal Palace and the Jemaa el Fna, the residential Riad Zitoun el Kedim and Riad Zitoun el Jedid quarters are home to two interesting museums and the beautiful Bahia Palace.

## DAR SI SAID

Derb Si Said, off Rue Riad Zitoun el Jedid. Daily except Tues 9am–4.45pm. 10dh. MAP P.62–63, POCKET MAP C13

A pleasing building, with beautiful pooled courtyards, scented with lemons, palms and flowers, the Dar Si Said was built in the late nineteenth century as a palace for the brother of Bou Ahmed (see opposite) who, like Bou Ahmed himself, became royal chamberlain. It houses the impressive **Museum of Moroccan Arts**, which is particularly strong on eighteenth- and nineteenth-century woodwork, including furniture, Berber doors and window frames, and wonderful painted ceilings. There are also (upstairs) a number of traditional wedding **palanquins**, and an early eleventh-century **marble basin** from the Andalusian capital Córdoba, decorated with what seem to be heraldic eagles and griffins. Not all of these will necessarily be on show at any one time.

## MAISON TISKIWIN

Derb el Bahia, off Rue Riad Zitoun el Jedid. Daily 9.30am–12.30pm & 2.30–6pm. 20dh. MAP P.62–63, POCKET MAP C13

The Maison Tiskiwin houses a collection of Moroccan and

DAR SI SAID

Saharan artefacts from the collection of Dutch anthropologist Bert Flint, which illustrate the cultural links across the desert resulting from the **caravan trade** between Morocco and Mali. Each room features carpets, fabrics, clothes and jewellery from a different region of the Sahara, with translations in English.

## THE BAHIA PALACE

Rue Riad Zitoun el Jedid. Daily 9am–4.30pm. 10dh. MAP P.62–63, POCKET MAP H6

The Bahia Palace – its name means "brilliance" – was originally built in 1866–67 for the then grand vizier (akin to a prime minister), **Si Moussa**. In the 1890s it was extended by his son, **Bou Ahmed**, himself a grand vizier and regent to the sultan, who ascended the throne aged 14. There is a certain pathos to the empty, echoing chambers of the palace, and the inevitable passing of Bou Ahmed's influence and glory. When he died, the palace was looted by its staff, and his family driven out to starvation and ruin.

You enter the palace from the west, through an arcaded courtyard. This leads to a small riad (enclosed garden), part of Bou Ahmed's extension and decorated with beautiful carved stucco and cedarwood surrounds. The adjoining eastern salon leads through to the **great courtyard** of Si Moussa's palace, with a fountain in its centre and vestibules on all sides, each boasting a marvellous painted wooden ceiling.

South of the great courtyard is the large riad, the heart of Si Moussa's palace, fragrant with fruit trees and melodious with birdsong, approaching the very ideal of beauty in Arabic domestic architecture. The halls to the east and west are decorated with fine zellij fireplaces and painted wooden ceilings. You leave the palace via the private apartment built for Ahmed's wife, **Lalla Zinab**, where again it's worth looking up to check out the painted ceiling, carved stucco and stained-glass windows.

## PLACE DES FERBLANTIERS

MAP P.62–63, POCKET MAP H7

This tinsmiths' square, once part of a souk belonging to the Mellah (see p.64), is now dominated by the workshops of **lantern makers** (see p.68). The remainder of the Mellah's souk can be found through a doorway just to the northeast.

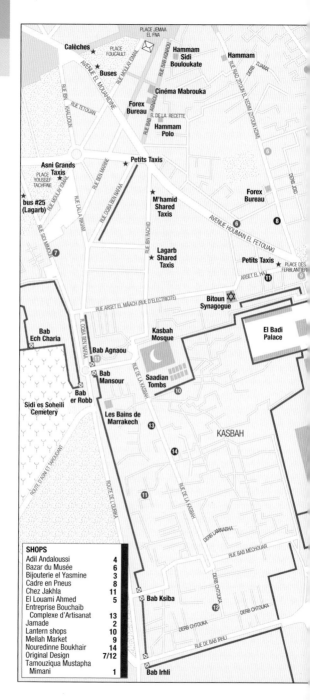

PLACE JEMAA EL FNA

Calèches

PLACE FOUCAULT

Hammam Sidi Bouloukate

Hammam

Buses

Cinéma Mabrouka

Forex Bureau

R. DE LA RECETTE

Hammam Polo

Asni Grands Taxis

PLACE YOUSSEF TACHFINE

Petits Taxis

bus #25 (Lagarb)

M'hamid Shared Taxis

Forex Bureau

AVENUE HOUMAN EL FETOUAKI

Lagarb Shared Taxis

Petits Taxis

PLACE DES FERBLANTIERS

ARSET EL HA

RUE ARSET EL MÄACH (RUE D'ELECTRICITÉ)

Bitoun Synagogue

Bab Ech Charia

Kasbah Mosque

El Badi Palace

Bab Agnaou

Bab Mansour

Saadian Tombs

Bab er Robb

Sidi es Soheili Cemetery

Les Bains de Marrakech

KASBAH

ROUTE D'ASNI ET IMOUZZAR

ROUTE DE L'OURIKA

RUE DE LA KASBAH

DERB LAKNABHA

RUE BAB MECHOUAR

Bab Ksiba

DERB CHTOUKA

DERB CHTOUKA

DERB CHTOUKA

RUE DE BAB IRHLI

Bab Irhli

RUE MOULAY ISMAIL
AVENUE EL MOUAHIDINE
RUE EL KHALDOUN
RUE BEN TETOUAN
RUE BAB AGNAOU
RUE RIAD ZITOUN EL KEDIM
ZITOUN KDIM
DERB DJAMA
DERB JDID
RUE BEN MARINE
RUE OGBA BEN NAFFA
RUE L'AILA BWAM
RUE BEN RACHID
RUE SIDI MIMOUN
RUE OGBA BEN NAFFA

**SHOPS**

| | |
|---|---|
| Adil Andaloussi | 4 |
| Bazar du Musée | 6 |
| Bijouterie el Yasmine | 3 |
| Cadre en Pneus | 8 |
| Chez Jakhla | 11 |
| El Louami Ahmed | 5 |
| Entreprise Bouchaib Complexe d'Artisanat | 13 |
| Jamade | 2 |
| Lantern shops | 10 |
| Mellah Market | 9 |
| Nouredinne Boukhair | 14 |
| Original Design | 7/12 |
| Tamouziqua Mustapha Mimani | 1 |

# The Southern Medina and Agdal Gardens

N

Dar Si Said

Maison Tiskiwin

Hammam Ziani

Bahia Palace

Bab Ghmat Cemetery

Mellah Market

Lazama Synagogue

Miâara Jewish Cemetery

Bab Berrima

MELLAH

BERRIMA

Royal Palace

Berrima Mosque

Bab er Ryal

BAB HMAR

RUE DE BAB HMAR

Exterior Mechouar

Interior Mechouar

Bab Agdal

Bab Laghdar

Grand Mechouar

Agdal Gardens

| CAFÉS | |
|---|---|
| Café El Badia | 9 |
| Un Déjeuner à Marrakech | 3 |

| PATISSERIE | |
|---|---|
| Patisserie Bab Agnaou | 11 |

| RESTAURANTS | |
|---|---|
| Dar Essalam | 6 |
| Dar Mima | 5 |
| El Bahia | 7 |
| Jama | 2 |
| Kosybar | 10 |
| Le Tanjia | 8 |
| Palais Gharnata | 4 |
| Pepe Nero | 1 |

| ACCOMMODATION | |
|---|---|
| Dar les Cigognes | 9 |
| La Sultana | 10 |
| Le Clos des Arts | 3 |
| Les Jardins de la Medina | 12 |
| Riad & Spa Bahia Salam | 6 |
| Riad Aguerzame | 1 |
| Riad Akka | 4 |
| Riad Bayti | 8 |
| Riad Dar One | 5 |
| Riad Jonan | 11 |
| Riyad al Moussika | 2 |
| Villa des Orangers | 7 |

0    100
metres

## THE MELLAH

MAP P.62–63, POCKET MAP G7–J7

Set up in 1558, Marrakesh's **Jewish ghetto** was almost a town in itself in the sixteenth century, presided over by rabbis, and possessing its own souks, gardens, fountains and synagogues. Today it is almost entirely Muslim – most of the Jews left long ago for Casablanca, France or Israel.

The quarter is immediately distinct, with taller houses and narrower streets than elsewhere in the Medina. Would-be guides may offer (for a tip, of course) to show you some of the surviving synagogues, notably the **Lazama** at 36 Derb Ragraga (no sign, just knock on the door; open to the public Sun–Thurs 9am–6pm, Fri 9am–1pm, closed Sat & Jewish hols; there's no charge, but a tip is expected). The synagogue is still in use but the interior is modern and not tremendously interesting. Like all the Mellah's synagogues, it forms part of a private house, which you'll notice is decorated with Star-of-David zellij tiling. Just outside the Mellah, on Rue Arset el Mâach (Rue de l'Electricité), the first-floor **Bitoun Synagogue** is out of use and closed to the public, but it's worth checking out the unusual mustard-yellow exterior, with a Star of David motif.

The **Miâara Jewish cemetery** on the east side of the Mellah (Sun–Thurs 8am–5pm, Fri 8am–1pm, closed Sat & Jewish hols; no charge but tip expected) is reckoned to date from the early seventeenth century. Among the tombs are eleven shrines to Jewish *marabouts* (*tzadikim*), illustrating an interesting parallel between the Moroccan varieties of Judaism and Islam.

## EL BADI PALACE

Bab Berrima. Daily 9am–4.45pm. 10dh.
MAP P.62–63, POCKET MAP G7

Though largely ruined, and reduced throughout to its red *pisé* walls, enough remains of Sultan Ahmed el Mansour's sixteenth-century El Badi Palace to suggest that its name – "**The Incomparable**" – was not entirely immodest. The main courtyard that you see today was the ceremonial part of the palace complex, built for the reception of ambassadors

EL BADI PALACE

and dignitaries, and not meant for everyday living.

The original entrance was in the southeast corner, but today you enter from the north, through the **Green Pavilion**, emerging into a vast **central courtyard** over 130m long and nearly as wide. In the northeast corner, you can climb up to get an overview from the ramparts and a closer view of the **storks** nesting atop them.

The central courtyard has four **sunken gardens**, each pair separated by a pool, with smaller pools in the four corners. When filled – as during the June Festival des Arts Populaires (see p.130) – they are an incredibly majestic sight.

You can pay another 10dh (at the main entrance) to see the original **minbar** (pulpit) from the Koutoubia Mosque (see p.36), housed in a pavilion in the southwest corner of the main courtyard. Once one of the most celebrated works of art in the Muslim world, it was commissioned from Córdoba, the Andalusian capital, in 1137 ("al-Andalus" or Andalusia was under Islamic rule and had close links to Morocco from 711 until 1492; it was also the Islamic world's main artistic centre). The *minbar* took eight years to complete, and was covered with the most exquisite inlay work of which, sadly, only patches remain. South of the courtyard are the ruins of the **palace stables** and, beyond them, leading towards the walls of the present Royal Palace, a series of **dungeons**, used as a prison into the twentieth century.

As Ahmed's court jester quipped at the palace's inauguration, "Sire, this will make a magnificent ruin!"

SUMMER PAVILION, AGDAL GARDENS

## AGDAL GARDENS

Access via the path leading south from the Interior Mechouar; bus #6 from Av Mohammed V near the Koutoubia will take you to the path's southern end, or take a taxi. Fri & Sun 9am–5pm. Free. MAP P.62–63, POCKET MAP H8–J9

These massive gardens, which stretch south for some 3km, are surrounded by walls, with gates (which are kept closed) at each of the northern corners. Inside, the orange, fig, lemon, apricot and pomegranate **orchards** are divided up by raised walkways and broad avenues of olive trees. The area is watered by a system of wells and **underground channels**, known as *khettara*, that go as far as the foothills of the Atlas and date, in part, from the very founding of the city, though the walls were not added until the nineteenth century.

At the heart of the gardens lies a series of pools, the largest of which is the **Sahraj el Hana**, the Tank of Health (now a green, algae-clogged rectangle of water). Probably dug during Almohad times, the pool is flanked by a ramshackle old **summer pavilion**, where the last few pre-colonial sultans held picnics and boating parties.

## KASBAH MOSQUE

Place des Tombeaux Saadiens. MAP P.62–63. POCKET MAP G7

Originally Almohad, but rebuilt in the sixteenth century, the minaret of this mosque, with its wonderful green *darj w ktarf*, gives an idea of what the Koutoubia must have looked like in its heyday, when its stonework was covered by plaster and paint. Only Muslims may enter, but everybody can admire the exterior.

## THE SAADIAN TOMBS

Rue de la Kasbah. Daily 9am–4.45pm. 10dh. MAP P.62–63, POCKET MAP G7

The tombs of the Saadians – the dynasty that ruled Morocco from 1554 to 1669 – escaped plundering by the rapacious Sultan Moulay Ismail, of the subsequent Alaouite dynasty, probably because he feared bad luck if he desecrated them. Instead, he blocked all access bar an obscure entrance from the Kasbah Mosque. The tombs lay half-ruined and half-forgotten until they were rediscovered by a French aerial survey in 1917.

SAADIAN TOMBS

The finer of the two **mausoleums** in the enclosure is on the left as you come in – a beautiful group of three rooms. Architecturally, the most important feature here is the **mihrab**, its pointed horseshoe arch supported by an incredibly delicate arrangement of columns. The room itself was originally an oratory, probably not intended for burial use. Opposite the mihrab, an elaborate arch leads to the domed central chamber and the tomb of Sultan Ahmed el Mansour, flanked by those of his sons and successors. The room is spectacular, with faint light filtering onto the tombs from an interior lantern placed in the tremendous vaulted roof, and the zellij tilework on the walls full of colour and motion. It was Ahmed who built the other mausoleum, older and less impressive, above the tombs of his mother and of the Saadian dynasty's founder, Mohammed el Sheikh. Outside, round the garden and courtyard, are scattered the tombs of over a hundred more Saadian princes and members of the royal household.

The best time to visit is early in the morning, before the crowds arrive, or late in the afternoon when they – and the heat – have largely gone.

## BAB AGNAOU

MAP P.62–63, POCKET MAP F7

This was one of the two original entrances to the Kasbah, but the magnificent blue granite gateway that stands here today was built in 1885. The entrance is surrounded by concentric arches of decoration and topped with an inscription in decorative script, which translates as: "Enter with blessing, serene people."

# Shops

### ADIL ANDALOUSSI

58 Riad Zitoun El Jedid ☎ 0638 886932, Ⓦ tamaroc.com. Daily 10am–9pm. MAP P.63

Adil sells only his own work, and only he sells it: hand tooled leather bags and babouches, and you can pop into his shop to see him at work. He's got some ready-made items in case you need them right away, but if you have the time, he'll make you a pair of babouches to order or a bag to your specifications, and at 200dh for the shoes or 250dh upwards for a bag, you can hardly complain about the price.

### BAZAR DU MUSÉE

38 Riad Zitoun El Jedid ☎ 0671 842628. Daily 10am–6pm. MAP P.63

Abdelkarim el Azri, who runs this shop, is a bit of a jack of all trades, and he's got anything from babouches to scarfs if you want to buy them at "I make you very good price my friend" -type rates; however, what you really come here for are the range of tea glasses, from cheap and cheerful mass-produced to hand-blown in Majorelle blue (that is, the colour of the pavillion in the Majorelle Garden; see p.72). He decorates many of these in hand-applied metal gilt, and if you need a pot to brew up in, he's got a few old ones for sale too.

### BIJOUTERIE EL YASMINE

68 Rue Riad Zitoun el Jedid ☎ 0663 260111. Daily 10am–7pm. MAP P.62–63, POCKET MAP C13

This unassuming little shop has some interesting and unusual enamelled jewellery and cutlery in striking colours, mainly striped. Pieces include earrings, pendants, key rings, teaspoons, salad spoons and cake knives. The cutlery, with its striped handles, is particularly attractive.

ARTEFACTS MADE FROM RECYCLED TYRES

### CADRE EN PNEUS

97 Rue Riad Zitoun el Kedim. Sat–Thurs 9am–6.30pm, Fri 9am–1pm. MAP P.62–63, POCKET MAP G7

This is one of a group of small shops at the southern end of this street that recycle disused car tyres. Initially they made hammam supplies such as buckets and flip-flops (the shops 20m further down towards Pl des Ferblantiers are better for these), but they've since branched out into products such as picture frames and framed mirrors – odd rather than elegant in black rubber, but certainly worth a look. Best buys are the tuffets (stools), which rather resemble giant liquorice allsorts.

### CHEZ JAKHA

29 Arset el Haj. Sat–Thurs 9am–8pm. MAP P.62–63, POCKET MAP G7

The walls and floor here are stacked solid with CDs and cassettes of local and foreign sounds. There's Algerian *raï* and Egyptian pop, as well as homegrown *raï* and *chaabi* (folk music), classical Andalusian music originally from Muslim-era Spain, religious music and even Moroccan hip-hop.

## EL LOUAMI AHMED

218 Rue Riad Zitoun el Jedid ☎ 0662 778347. Daily 10am–8pm. MAP P.62–63, POCKET MAP C13

If the leather babouches in the main souk don't wow you, here's a whole different concept: women's babouches made from raffia straw, mainly candy-coloured, and there are ladies' sandals too. Ahmed sits in the shop making them by hand, so you can see him at work. A pair of simple babouches costs 150–300dh.

## ENTREPRISE BOUCHAIB COMPLEXE D'ARTISANAT

7 Derb Baissi Kasbah, Rue de la Kasbah ☎ 0524 381853, ⊛ complexeartisanal.com. Daily 8.30am–7pm. MAP P.62–63, POCKET MAP G8

A massive craftwork depart-ment store with a huge range of goods at (supposedly) fixed prices, only slightly higher than in the souks. The sales assistants who follow you round are generally quite charming and informative. Carpets are the best buy, at around 4000dh for a decent-sized killim, or 7000dh for a knotted carpet. There's also a huge selection of

LANTERNS ON PLACE DES FERBLANTIERS

jewellery, ceramics, brassware and even furniture.

## JAMADE

1 Pl Douar Graoua, Rue Riad Zitoun el Jedid ☎ 0524 429042. Daily 10.30am–7pm, Tues–Thurs & Sun till 10pm. MAP P.62–63, POCKET MAP C13

A chic little shop selling modern ceramics, as well as dresses, hats, bags and purses by local designers and co-ops, some interesting jewellery and some rather overpriced beauty products and perfumes. Best is their modern, designer take on the traditional Moroccan tea glass.

## LANTERN SHOPS

Pl des Ferblantiers. Daily 8am–7pm. MAP P.62–63, POCKET MAP H7

The stores on the eastern side of the square sell a big selection of brass and iron lanterns in all shapes and sizes, some with coloured glass panels, which make excellent light shades for electric bulbs. The many-pointed star-shaped lanterns with glass panes are a big favourite, as are simple candle-holder lanterns. There are larger and grander designs too, and these shops don't only sell them, but also make the lanterns on the premises, so you can watch the lantern makers at work.

## MELLAH MARKET

Off Derb Jedid, by Pl des Ferblantiers. Daily 9am–7pm. MAP P.62–63, POCKET MAP H7

This is an interesting little market, especially for spices, which are piled up in attractively multicoloured and very photogenic pyramids. Other shops offer bowlfuls of glutinous traditional soap or rolls of rich fabric. Along with the rest of the Mellah, the market is now being given something of a facelift.

### TAMOUZIQUA MUSTAPHA MIMANI

84 Kennaria Teoula, off Rue Riad Zitoun el Jedid ☎ 0671 518724. Daily 9am–8pm. MAP P.62–63, POCKET MAP C12

This small shop specializes in Moroccan musical instruments, most notably drums, which they make themselves in their neighbouring workshop, and Gnaoua castanets. Also on sale are lute-like *ginbris*, which make excellent souvenirs to hang on your wall back home.

# Cafés

### CAFÉ EL BADIA

Off Pl des Ferblantiers, by Bab Berrima ☎ 0524 389975. Daily 9am–10pm. MAP P.62–63, POCKET MAP H7

On a rooftop looking out over Place des Ferblantiers and towards the Mellah, this is one place to get close to the storks nesting on the walls of the El Badi Palace. It serves a range of hot and cold (non-alcoholic) drinks, and set menus (80–120dh, including one vegetarian) featuring soup, salad, couscous, and Moroccan sweetmeats for afters.

### UN DÉJEUNER À MARRAKECH

2–4 Pl Douar Graoua, Rue Riad Zitoun el Jedid ☎ 0524 378387. Daily 11am–10pm. MAP P.62–63, POCKET MAP C13

Cool upmarket tearoom and restaurant serving teas and infusions, salads – and we're talking Caesar salad or beef carpaccio, nothing common or garden – and snacks (sandwiches, savoury tarts, even crêpes). They also offer the odd main dish, usually involving a fusion of some kind, such as beef brochettes with stir-fried veg and sushi rice, and daily specials, generally in the 90–140dh range.

### NOUREDINNE BOUKHAIR

305 Rue de la Kasbah. Daily 10am–10pm. MAP P.62–63, POCKET MAP G8

This is the best among a handful of shops on this stretch of the street (there are imitators at nos. 315 and 297) that sell jolly little paintings on the wooden boards used by students in Koranic schools. They aren't exactly high art, but they're bright, breezy and original, and prices start around 100dh.

### ORIGINAL DESIGN

231 Rue Riad Zitoun el Jedid & 47 Pl des Ferblantiers ☎ 0524 383705. Daily 9am–7.30pm. MAP P.62–63, POCKET MAP C13 & H7

They started off making ceramics, but that now takes second place to purses, handbags and tasselled towels, not to mention glass tea sets. The designs are unmistakeably Moroccan in inspiration, but all with a modern touch, setting them apart from the run-of-the-mill versions elsewhere.

# Patisserie

### PATISSERIE BAB AGNAOU

Bab Agnaou. Daily 9am–9pm. MAP P.62–63,
POCKET MAP F7

Little more than a hole in
the wall, actually in the gate
(Bab Agnaou) itself, this little
patisserie serves nothing
fancy, just good, traditional
Moroccan sticky delights,
mostly involving nuts and filo
pastry fried in syrup on the
premises. Even if you don't
want to buy a kilo of them,
a triangular *briouat* (filo
parcel, in this case of nuts),
perfumed with orange
blossom water, is irresistible,
and a snip at just 3dh.

# Restaurants

### DAR ESSALAM

170 Rue Riad Zitoun el Kedim
☎ 0524 443520, ⊛ daressalam.com. Daily
11.45am–11.45pm. MAP P.62–63,
POCKET MAP C13

This seventeenth-century
mansion has five different
salons, all beautifully done out
and dripping with zellij and
stucco. Winston Churchill and
Sean Connery are among the
past diners here, and Doris
Day and James Stewart also
ate here in Hitchcock's *The
Man Who Knew Too Much*.
The food (*menus* 250–330dh
plus wine) is good, the
ambience superb, and in the
evening there are musicians,
belly-dancers and Moroccan
Berber dancers.

### DAR MIMA

9 Derb Zaouia el Khadiria, off Rue Riad
Zitoun el Jedid ☎ 0524 385252. Daily except
Wed 8pm–midnight. MAP P.62–63, POCKET MAP C13

A modest nineteenth-century
townhouse converted into a
simple but comfortable
restaurant with the sort of
food and ambience that you
might find in a well-to-do
Marrakshi family home. The
*menu* is 220dh per person
plus wine.

### EL BAHIA

1 Rue Riad Zitoun el Jedid, by the Bahia
Palace ☎ 0524 378679. Daily noon–3pm &
7–11pm. MAP P.62–63, POCKET MAP C13

A proper palace restaurant,
but with a bargain-priced
150–300dh set menu. It's
housed in a beautifully
restored mansion, complete
with finely carved stucco and
painted wooden ceilings,
which used to offer meals
with a floorshow at three
times the price.

### JAMA

149 Rue Riad Zitoun el Jedid ☎ 0524 429872.
Daily noon–4pm & 6.30–10pm. MAP P.62–63,
POCKET MAP C12

A quiet little patio, lit up with
candles in the evening,
serving a small selection of
well-cooked and modestly
priced (50–60dh) traditional
tajines, including lamb or beef
with figs or prunes, and
chicken with lemons and
olives, followed by their own
house yoghurt.

## KOSYBAR

47 Pl des Ferblantiers ☎ 0524 380324, Ⓦ kosybar.com. Daily 11am–1am (salads and drinks served 11am–midnight). MAP P.62–63, POCKET MAP H7

A stylish restaurant and bar with upstairs terraces overlooking Place des Ferblantiers. At lunchtime (until 4pm) there's a 150dh set menu or light but exotic dishes such as cabbage stuffed with Chinese mushrooms, and in the evening a full à la carte menu with offerings such as a seafood tajine or roast duck breast with black olives and fig jam, or you can go for a lighter option in the form of sushi. Main dishes go for around 60–90dh at midday, 150–180dh in the evening.

## LE TANJIA

14 Derb Jedid, by Pl des Ferblantiers ☎ 0524 383836. Daily 11am–3pm & 7pm–midnight. MAP P.62–63, POCKET MAP H7

Stylish bar-restaurant, billed as an "oriental brasserie", serving well-cooked Moroccan dishes (including vegetarian options) in an old mansion with modern decor. It's not outrageously expensive – count on around 300dh per head plus wine.

## PALAIS GHARNATA

5–6 Derb el Arsa, off Rue Riad Zitoun el Jedid ☎ 0524 389615, Ⓦ gharnata.com. Daily 8–11pm. MAP P.62–63, POCKET MAP H6

This place is popular with foreign visitors, though

LE TANJIA

unfortunately the food (the 550dh *menu* features pastilla, couscous, lamb tajine and wine) is merely so-so, and individual diners play second fiddle to groups. However, the sixteenth-century mansion is magnificently decorated, with an Italian alabaster fountain at its centre; scenes from *The Return of the Pink Panther* were shot here. Past patrons have included Jacqueline Kennedy. There's a floorshow (music and dancing) from 8.30pm.

## PEPE NERO

Riyad al Moussika, 17 Derb Cherkaoui (off Rue Douar Graoua) ☎ 0524 389067, Ⓦ pepenero-marrakech.com. Daily noon–2.30pm & 7.30–11pm. MAP P.62–63, POCKET MAP C12

The terrace and lounge of the *Riyad al Moussika* make an elegant venue for this classy restaurant, serving fine Moroccan and Italian food, accompanied by Moroccan and Italian wines. There's a Moroccan menu and an Italian one, and you can pick and mix, but the Italian dishes are generally the best. Main dishes 160–250dh.

KOSYBAR

# The Ville Nouvelle and Palmery

The downtown area of Marrakesh's new town, the Ville Nouvelle, is Guéliz, whose main thoroughfare, Avenue Mohammed V, runs all the way down to the Koutoubia. It's in Guéliz that you'll find the more upmarket shops and most of Marrakesh's nightlife. South of Guéliz, the Hivernage district was built as a garden suburb, and is where most of the city's newer tourist hotels are located. Though the Ville Nouvelle is hardly chock-a-block with attractions, it does have one must-see: the Majorelle Garden, which is beautifully laid out with lily ponds, cactuses and a striking blue pavilion. West of Hivernage, the Menara gardens are larger, greener and more like a park. Otherwise, you can get some peace and respite from the full-on activity of Marrakesh's streets by heading to the Palmery, or oasis, just outside the city.

## MAJORELLE GARDEN (JARDIN BOU SAF)

Rue Yves Saint-Laurent (off Av Yacoub el Mansour) ⓦ jardinmajorelle.com. Daily: May–Sept 8am–6pm; Oct–April 8am–5.30pm; Ramadan 9am–5pm. 50dh; no dogs or unaccompanied children allowed. MAP P.73, POCKET MAP D2

The Majorelle Garden is a meticulously planned twelve-acre botanical garden, created in the 1920s and 1930s by French painter **Jacques Majorelle** (1886–1962), and subsequently owned by fashion designer **Yves Saint Laurent**. The feeling of tranquillity here is enhanced by verdant groves of bamboo, dwarf palm and agave, the cactus garden and the various lily-covered pools. The **pavilion** is painted in a striking cobalt blue – the colour of French workmen's overalls, so Majorelle claimed, though it seems to have improved in the Moroccan light.

The pavilion (25dh), Majorelle's studio, is now a Berber Museum, displaying traditional Berber crafts such as textiles and carpets, costumes and jewellery, and even an old wooden mosque pulpit.

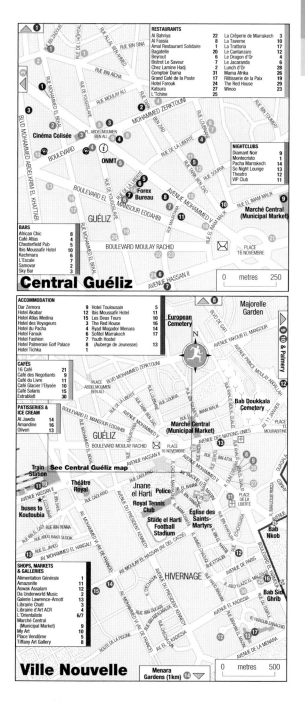

## Central Guéliz

**RESTAURANTS**

| | |
|---|---|
| Al Bahriya | 22 |
| Al Fassia | 8 |
| Amal Restaurant Solidaire | 1 |
| Bagatelle | 20 |
| Beyrout | 6 |
| Bistrot Le Saveur | 7 |
| Chez Lamine Hadj | 2 |
| Comptoir Darna | 31 |
| Grand Café de la Poste | 17 |
| Hotel Farouk | 24 |
| Katsura | 27 |
| L'tchine | 25 |
| La Crêperie de Marrakech | 3 |
| La Taverne | 10 |
| La Trattoria | 17 |
| Le Cantanzaro | 12 |
| Le Dragon d'Or | 4 |
| Le Jacaranda | 6 |
| Lunch d'Or | 28 |
| Mama Afrika | 26 |
| Rôtisserie de la Paix | 19 |
| The Red House | 29 |
| Winoo | 23 |

**NIGHTCLUBS**

| | |
|---|---|
| Diamant Noir | 9 |
| Montecristo | 1 |
| Pacha Marrakech | 14 |
| So Night Lounge | 13 |
| Theatro | 12 |
| VIP Club | 11 |

**BARS**

| | |
|---|---|
| African Chic | 8 |
| Café Atlas | 4 |
| Chesterfield Pub | 9 |
| Ibis Moussafir Hotel | 10 |
| Kechmara | 6 |
| L'Escale | 5 |
| Samovar | 7 |
| Sky Bar | 3 |

Cinéma Colisée
ONMT
Forex Bureau
GUÉLIZ
Marché Central (Municipal Market)
PLACE 16 NOVEMBRE

0 metres 250

## Ville Nouvelle

**ACCOMMODATION**

| | | | |
|---|---|---|---|
| Dar Zemora | 9 | Hotel Toulousain | 5 |
| Hotel Akabar | 12 | Ibis Moussafir Hotel | 10 |
| Hotel Atlas Medina | 15 | Les Deux Tours | 10 |
| Hotel des Voyageurs | 3 | The Red House | 16 |
| Hotel du Pacha | 4 | Ryad Mogador Menara | 14 |
| Hotel Farouk | 6 | Sofitel Marrakech | 17 |
| Hotel Fashion | 7 | Youth Hostel | |
| Hotel Palmeraie Golf Palace | 8 | (Auberge de Jeunesse) | 13 |
| Hotel Tichka | 1 | | |

**CAFÉS**

| | |
|---|---|
| 16 Café | 21 |
| Café des Negotiants | 9 |
| Café du Livre | 11 |
| Café Glacier l'Elysée | 11 |
| Café Solaris | 15 |
| Extrablatt | 30 |

**PATISSERIES & ICE CREAM**

| | |
|---|---|
| Al Jawda | 14 |
| Amandine | 16 |
| Oliveri | 13 |

**SHOPS, MARKETS & GALLERIES**

| | |
|---|---|
| Alimentation Générale | 1 |
| Amazonite | 11 |
| Aswak Assalam | 12 |
| Da Underworld Music | 2 |
| Galerie Lawrence-Arnott | 13 |
| Librairie Chatr | 3 |
| Librairie d'Art ACR | 4 |
| L'Orientaliste | 6/7 |
| Marché Central (Municipal Market) | 9 |
| My Art | 10 |
| Place Vendôme | 5 |
| Tiffany Art Gallery | 8 |

Majorelle Garden
European Cemetery
Bab Doukkala Cemetery
Marché Central (Municipal Market)
GUÉLIZ
PLACE 16 NOVEMBRE
PLACE ABDELMOUMEN BEN ALI
PLACE EL MOURABITINE
PLACE DE LA LIBERTÉ
Bab Nkob
Train Station
See Central Guéliz map
Théâtre Royal
Jnane el Harti
Police
Royal Tennis Club
Stade el Harti Football Stadium
Église des Saints-Martyrs
buses to Koutoubia
HIVERNAGE
Bab Sid Ghrib
& Palmery

Menara Gardens (1km)

0 metres 500

## MENARA GARDENS

Av de la Menara. Daily 8am–5pm. Free.
MAP P.73, POCKET MAP A8–A9

A popular picnic spot for Marrakshi families, the Menara gardens couldn't be simpler to find: just follow the road from Bab Jedid, the gateway by the *Hotel La Mamounia*. The gardens are centred on a rectangular **pool** that provides a classic postcard image against a backdrop of the High Atlas mountains. Like the Adgal Gardens (see p.65), the Menara was restored and its pavilions rebuilt in the mid-nineteenth century, though unlike the Agdal it is more olive grove than orchard. The poolside **Minzah** pavilion (daily 9am–5pm; 10dh) replaced an earlier Saadian structure.

The gardens are served by bus #11 from the Koutoubia. There's usually someone by the park entrance offering camel rides for those wanting a little spin.

## AVENUE MOHAMMED V

MAP P.73, POCKET MAP B3–D5

Named after the king who presided over Morocco's independence from France, Avenue Mohammed V is

Marrakesh's main artery. It's on and around this boulevard that you'll find the city's main concentration of upmarket shops, restaurants and smart pavement cafés, and its junctions form the Ville Nouvelle's main centres of activity: **Place de la Liberté**, with its modern fountain; **Place 16 Novembre**, by the main post office; and **Place Abdelmoumen Ben Ali**, epicentre of Marrakesh's modern shopping zone. Looking back along Avenue Mohammed V from Guéliz to the Medina, on a clear day at least, you should see the Koutoubia rising in the distance.

## ÉGLISE DES SAINTS-MARTYRS

Rue de l'Imam Ali ☎ 0524 430585. Mon–Sat 6–7.30pm & Sun 10am–noon. Free. MAP P.73, POCKET MAP C5

Marrakesh's **Catholic church**, built in 1930, could easily be a little church in rural France but for its distinctly Marrakshi red-ochre hue. The church is dedicated to six Franciscan friars who insisted on preaching Christianity on the city's streets in the year 1220. When the sultan ordered them to either desist or leave, they refused, and were promptly beheaded, to be canonized by the Church in 1481.

## THÉÂTRE ROYAL

40 Av Mohammed VI ☎ 0524 431516. Daily 9am–8pm. Free. MAP P.73, POCKET MAP B4

With its Classical portico and dome, designed by Morocco's leading architect, **Charles Boccara**, this is the most impressive piece of new architecture in the Ville Nouvelle. As well as a theatre, it has a hall exhibiting paintings and sculpture by local artists.

## THE EUROPEAN CEMETERY

Rue Erraouda. Daily: April–Sept 7am–7pm; Oct–March 8am–6pm. Free.
MAP P.73, POCKET MAP C2

Opened in 1925, this is a peaceful plot with lots of wild flowers, and some quite Poe-esque French family mausoleums. The first thing you'll notice on entry is the large white obelisk dedicated to the soldiers who fell fighting in Africa for Free France and democracy during World War II; 333 of these men have their last resting places in the cemetery's section H. The oldest part, to the left of the

obelisk as you come in, contains the tombs of colonists from the 1920s and 1930s, most of whom seem to have been under forty years old when they died.

## THE PALMERY

5km northeast of town, between the Route de Fès (N8) and the Route de Casablanca (N9). MAP P.73, POCKET MAP J1

Marrakesh's **Palmery** is dotted with the villas of prosperous Marrakshis, and also boasts a golf course and a couple of luxury hotels. The clumps of date palms look rather windswept, but the Palmery does have a certain tranquillity, and it's several degrees cooler than the Medina, which makes it a particular attraction in summer. Supposedly, it sprang from stones spat out by the date-munching troops of Marrakesh's founder, Youssef Ben Tachfine, but in fact the dates produced by its fifty thousand-odd palms are not of eating quality.

The most popular route through the oasis is the **Circuit de la Palmeraie**, which meanders through the trees and villas from the Route de Fès to the Route de Casablanca. The classic way to see it is by *calèche* (see p.122), and the sightseeing bus, the Marrakech Bus Touristique (see box, p.122), travels round it too. It's also possible to tour the Palmery on a camel – men by the roadside offer rides – or you could even do it on foot, though it's quite a long 5km stroll. As for public transport, the Route de Fès turn-off is served by bus #17, but the Route de Casablanca end is trickier, so it's best to take a cab up to that end to start, and finish at the Route de Fès, where there are more transport options.

# Shops, markets and galleries

## ALIMENTATION GÉNÉRALE

54 Av Mohammed V, at the corner of Rue Mohammed el Bekal, Guéliz ☎ 0524 447182. Daily 8.30am–noon & 2–8pm. MAP P.73, POCKET MAP A14

Forget the groceries – they're just a front for what this place really sells, which is booze. Among the spirits, the stuff in what looks like a Ricard bottle is popular locally, but best avoided. Moroccan wines, mostly red, are variable, but the top choices are CB or Chateau Roslane, at 200dh a bottle, followed by Medaillon (112dh) and Domaine de Sahari (60dh and 81dh). Among the cheap brands (45dh), Cabernet and Ksar are usually quite drinkable.

## AMAZONITE

94 Bd el Mansour Eddahbi, Guéliz ☎ 0524 449926. Mon–Sat 10am–1pm & 4–7.30pm. MAP P.73, POCKET MAP B15

The Marrakesh branch of a Casablanca shop long known for its fine stock of *objets d'art*, Amazonite is the product of the owner's passion for rare and beautiful things. Most of the pieces are antique, with a hefty proportion comprising jewellery; if asked, staff will explain each item with charm and grace.

## ASWAK ASSALAM

Av 11 Janvier at the junction with Av Prince Moulay Abdallah, Guéliz ☎ 0524 431004. Daily 9am–11pm. MAP P.73, POCKET MAP E3

This smallish hypermarket may not be the most characterful shopping experience in town, but it is quick and easy. There's a good patisserie section, and serve-yourself grains and spices, so you can weigh out exactly how much you want. You'll also find a fuller (and probably fresher) range of commercial dairy products than you would at a grocery store, and there are even household items like kitchen ware, including couscous steamers.

## DA UNDERWORLD MUSIC

Rue Tarik Ben Ziad, Guéliz ☎ 0524 423881. Daily 11am–10pm. MAP P.73, POCKET MAP B14

A good selection of Moroccan and Arabic music, with lots of Gnaoua, *raï* and Moroccan dance and hip-hop CDs at 20dh a go. However, there's also a section for Western music, not exactly up-to-the-minute, and rarely underground, but you can still turn up some great bargains.

## GALERIE LAWRENCE-ARNOTT

Immeuble el Khalil, Av des Nations-Unies, Guéliz ☎ 0524 430999. Mon–Fri 10am–12.30pm & 3–7pm, Sat 10am–12.30pm. MAP P.73, POCKET MAP D4

Very upmarket gallery founded by two London art dealers, friends of Princess Diana and already well established on the London art scene when they opened a gallery in Tangier. This is their second Moroccan locale. The paintings and sculptures, as you might expect, are very fine and very expensive

AMAZONITE

(nothing under 5000dh), but if you want to see what's really big on the Moroccan art scene, this is the place to come.

## LIBRAIRIE CHATR

19 Av Mohammed V, Guéliz ☎ 0524 447997. Mon–Thurs 8.30am–1pm & 3–8pm, Fri 8.30–1pm & 3.30–8.30pm, Sat 8.30am–1pm & 4–8pm. MAP P.73, POCKET MAP A14

This bookshop and stationer sells mainly French titles, but there's also a shelf of English-language material, mostly classics, at the back on the right. The front part of the shop supplies artists' materials, including paint and brushes, as well as a large and varied selection of pens.

## LIBRAIRIE MENZIL EL FAN

Résidence Tayeb, 55 Bd Mohammed Zerktouni, Guéliz ☎ 0524 446792. Mon–Sat 9am–12.30pm & 3–7pm. MAP P.73, POCKET MAP A14

This bookshop stocks the beautiful ACR range of French art and coffee-table books, which include several on Marrakesh and Moroccan interior design. There are also books on subjects such as architecture, textiles and jewellery, and cooking (though mostly in French) and even greetings cards.

## L'ORIENTALISTE

11 & 15 Rue de la Liberté, Guéliz ☎ 0524 434074. Mon–Sat 9am–1pm & 3–7pm, Sun 9am–12.30pm. MAP P.73, POCKET MAP B14

Specializing in rather chic North African-style home furnishings (though some are actually Syrian), L'Orientaliste also does a fine line in limited Moroccan Pop Art screen-prints by local artist Hassan Hajjaj. At no. 11 the stock is mainly furniture, while at no. 15 they concentrate on smaller items and accessories, including glassware and their own perfume.

L'ORIENTALISTE

## MARCHÉ CENTRAL (MUNICIPAL MARKET)

Rue Ibn Toumert, Guéliz. Daily 7am–8pm, though shops within the market may keep shorter hours, and most close Fri or Sun. MAP P.73, POCKET MAP C4

A far cry from the souks in the Medina, this covered market is where expats and better-off Marrakshis come for their fresh fish, meat, fruit and veg. There are two butchers selling horsemeat, one selling pork, and shops specializing in pickled lemons, perfumed soaps, fossils, ceramics, booze, tourist tat and fresh flowers.

## MY ART

Rue Saint Aulaire by Pl 16 Novembre ☎ 0524 449181. Mon–Sat 9.30am–1.30pm & 3.30–7.30pm. MAP P.73

Modern art and design, all made in Marrakesh, with everything from sculpture and paintings to furniture, soft toys and decorative *objets d'art*. The shop is a cool exhibition space that's worth a look just to see what they've got. This is the modern, chic side of Marrakesh, a far cry from the traditional crafts on sale in the Medina, but actually just as exciting, and with fixed prices.

## PLACE VENDÔME

141 Av Mohammed V, Guéliz ☎ 0524 435263.
Mon-Sat 9am-1pm & 3-7.30pm. MAP P.73,
POCKET MAP B14

Morocco leather is world
famous, and you'll find
plenty of it here including
some very sumptuous soft
leather and suede, in the
form of bags, belts, wallets
and clothes. Small coin
purses start at 100dh, and
there are some very stylish
ladies' garments – jackets,
coats and dresses – at
around 3000dh.

## TIFFANY ART GALLERY

199 Av Mohammed V, Guéliz ☎ 0667 589900.
Mon-Sat 9.30am-12.30pm & 3.30-8.30pm.
MAP P.73, POCKET MAP B15

An airy space exhibiting some
of the latest up-and-coming
Moroccan artists and
sculptors on the scene. The
style is very much contemporary, but recognizably
local, with Marrakesh and
Morocco featuring strongly in
almost all of the paintings.
Prices are high, but certainly
not ridiculous.

PLACE VENDÔME

# Cafés

## 16 CAFÉ

Pl 16 Novembre, Guéliz ☎ 0524 339670,
ⓦ 16cafe.com. Daily 8am-11pm. MAP P.73,
POCKET MAP C4

There are coffees, teas and
infusions on offer at this cool,
elegant café, not to mention hot
chocolate, ice cream and
amazing pastries. It's located in
a modern shopping development, and the cuisine is even
more modern than the simple,
elegant decor. Breakfasts
(35–90dh) are served till noon,
after which you can get a main
dish of the day plus starter and
coffee for 200dh, and alcohol is
also served.

## CAFÉ DES NEGOTIANTS

Pl Abdelmoumen Ben Ali ☎ 0524 422345.
Daily 6am-midnight. MAP P.73

Slap bang on the busiest corner
in Guéliz, this grand café has
been going since 1936 and it's
*the* place to sit out on the
pavement and really feel that
you're in the heart of modern
Marrakesh. It's also an excellent
venue in which to spend the
morning over a coffee, with an
omelette (10dh) or sandwich
(23–35dh) to accompany your
caffeine fix.

## CAFÉ DU LIVRE

44 Rue Tarik Ben Ziad, by *Hotel Toulousain*,
Guéliz ☎ 0524 432149. Mon-Sat
10am-11.30pm. MAP P.73, POCKET MAP B14

A very elegant space, serving
tea and coffee, juices,
breakfasts, salads, sandwiches
and brochettes, even tapas
(well, mezze) at 25dh a go, or
a selection of three for 70dh
and toasties (25–30dh).
There's also draught beer.
Most importantly, the café has
a library of secondhand
English books to read or buy,
and free wi-fi too.

CAFÉ DU LIVRE

### CAFÉ GLACIER L'ÉLYSÉE

8 Bd Mohammed Zerktouni, next to the CTM office. Daily 5am–11pm. MAP P.73, POCKET MAP A14

You need only wander less than 200m off Avenue Mohammed V to slice a third off the price of your coffee, as you will if you eschew the glitzy cafés on the main thoroughfare in favour of this Moroccan coffee house. It's nothing special, but that's the point: the coffee's just as good, so are the croissants, and all that's missing is the chic, Frenchified ambience; but you never wanted that anyway, right?

### CAFÉ SOLARIS

170 Av Mohammed V ☎ 0524 423614. Daily 6am–11pm. MAP P.73, POCKET MAP B15

This bright establishment under a neon sign looks just a tad more modern and sophisticated than your average Marrakesh coffee house, with tiled floors and mirror panels behind the bar. The wicker chairs and tables are just right to relax at with your coffee and croissant (or tea, infusion, juice or light meal) while you watch the comings and goings along the boulevard. Set breakfasts go for 25–58dh.

### EXTRABLATT

Rue Echchouada, at the corner with Av el Kadissia, Hivernage ☎ 0524 435043. Daily 8am–midnight. MAP P.73, POCKET MAP D6

Spacious and slightly glitzy upmarket café with an outside terrace, the Marrakesh branch of a German franchise chain, where you can get a range of set breakfasts (45–90dh), sandwiches, salads, coffees, sodas, juices, mocktails and light meals, including a couple of vegetarian options. If you're in Hivernage, it's something of an oasis.

# Patisseries and ice cream

### AL JAWDA (CHEZ MME ALAWI)

11 Rue de la Liberté, Guéliz ☎ 0524 433897. Daily 8am–8.30pm. MAP P.73, POCKET MAP B15

A refined patisserie, patronized by Marrakesh's high society and expatriate community. A fine selection of mouthwatering Moroccan pastries are on offer, including almond-filled petits fours such as crescent-shaped *cornes de gazelle*. It's a bit pricey, but is also very good.

### AMANDINE

177 Rue Mohammed el Bekal, Guéliz ☎ 0524 449612, ⊕ amandinemarrakech.com. Daily 7am–9pm. MAP P.73, POCKET MAP A15

An elegant café-patisserie, stuffed full of scrumptious almond-filled Moroccan pastries and French-style cream cakes, where you can relax with a coffee and your choice of sweetmeat. The Moroccan sweets include *cornes de gazelle* (almond-filled crescents) and – their speciality – macaroons, in a variety of flavours, although they're admittedly a bit pricey at 200dh/kg. They even have pastillas (55dh for a one-person version).

## OLIVERI

Bd el Mansour Eddahbi, behind *Hotel Agdal*, Guéliz ☎ 0524 448913. Daily 8am–midnight. MAP P.73, POCKET MAP A15

The Marrakesh branch of a Casablanca firm that's been serving delicious, creamy, Italian-style ices since colonial times, this is the poshest ice-cream parlour in town. You can eat your scoop from a proper ice-cream goblet among elegant surroundings, accompanied, should you so desire, by coffee; or else you can take it away in a waffle cone.

# Restaurants

## AL BAHRIYA

75 Bis Bd Moulay Rachid, Guéliz ☎ 0661 242047. Daily 11am–midnight. MAP P.73, POCKET MAP B15

Very cheap and very popular fish restaurant, always crowded out at lunchtimes. For 50dh you get a big plate of hake, sole and squid, plus bread, olives and sauce, or for not much more there are swordfish brochettes, fish tajines, fried prawns and fish soup. Unbeatable value.

## AL FASSIA

Résidence Tayeb, 55 Bd Mohammed Zerktouni, Guéliz ☎ 0524 434060, ⓦ alfassia .com. Daily except Tues noon–2.30pm & 7.30–11pm. MAP P.73, POCKET MAP B14

*Al Fassia* is truly Moroccan – both in decor and cuisine – and specializes in dishes from the country's culinary capital, Fez. Start with that great Fassi classic, pigeon pastilla, followed by a choice of four different lamb tajines, or any of the other sumptuous Fassi offerings. Expect to pay around 350dh, more with wine. If you want to sample the very best traditional Moroccan cooking, with superb ambience and service, this is the place.

TAJINE AT AL FASSIA

## AMAL RESTAURANT SOLIDAIRE

Rue Allal Ben Ahmed at Rue Ibn Sina ☎ 0524 446896, ⓦ amalrestaurant.wordpress.com. Daily noon–4pm. MAP P.73, POCKET MAP A14

A non-profit self-help organiza-tion for disadvantaged women where training in the catering trade is put to good use in this lunchtime restaurant. What exactly's on offer changes from day to day, but there's always a tasty tajine (75–150dh), often couscous (150dh) and usually cakes and pastries too. You can also participate in a cookery workshop (daily except Fri 10am–noon), and then eat what you cooked.

## BAGATELLE

103 Rue Yougoslavie ☎ 0524 430274, ⓦ bagatelle-marrakech.com. Daily 10am–3pm & 7–11pm. MAP P.73, POCKET MAP A15

Photos of Marrakesh in the 1950s deck the walls, and there's a lovely vine-shaded garden to eat in at this French-style bistro which first opened its doors in 1949. You can start with an entrée such as pork and guinea fowl terrine, take in some braised veal tongue in caper sauce, and round it off with a refreshing sorbet. Throw in a coffee or a mint tea, and you'll be paying around 250dh per head.

## BEYROUT

10 Rue Loubnane, Guéliz ☎ 0524 423525. Daily noon–3pm & 7pm–midnight. MAP P.73, POCKET MAP B14

A Lebanese restaurant serving typical Middle Eastern cuisine, starting off, naturally, with cold mezze (hors d'oeuvres) such as hummus, *moutabbel* (aubergine and tahini dip) and tabbouleh, and hot starters such as falafel, *kubbe* (a fried bulgur wheat ball with a meat and onion filling), even moussaka. You can get a selection of eight mezze for 265dh, twelve for 390dh, and if you've still got room after that, mains go for 80–130dh. Licensed.

## BISTROT LE SAVEUR

*Le Caspien Hotel*, 12 Rue Loubnane, Guéliz ☎ 0524 422282. Daily noon–11pm. MAP P.73, POCKET MAP B14

Opposite the end of Rue de la Liberté, this is a modest little restaurant serving a selection of international dishes, mostly French or Moroccan, but there are also pizzas and even a few Thai dishes. All are good, and quite moderately priced, with main dishes at 120–180dh and a 120dh set menu. Licensed.

## CHEZ LAMINE

19 Résidence Yasmine, Rue Ibn Aïcha, corner with Rue Mohammed el Bekal, Guéliz ☎ 0524 431164. Daily 9am–11pm. MAP P.73, POCKET MAP A2

Unpretentious, inexpensive restaurant (main dishes 50–70dh) which is very popular with Marrakshis for *mechoui* (roasts), grills, tajines, sheep's head, brochettes and other indigenous, mainly lamb-based dishes.

## COMPTOIR DARNA

Rue Echchouada, Hivernage ☎ 0524 437702, Ⓦ comptoirmarrakech.com. Daily 7pm–3am (food served 8pm–1am). MAP P.73, POCKET MAP D6

Downstairs it's a restaurant serving reliably good Moroccan and international cuisine, with main courses at 145–245dh, and dishes such as seafood tajine, salmon steak or weeping tiger (steak in ginger sauce), as well as one or two vegetarian options. Upstairs it's a chic lounge bar, very popular with Marrakesh's young and rich. The bar opens at 7pm, with meals served from 8pm, and cabaret entertainment starting at 10.30pm.

## GRAND CAFÉ DE LA POSTE

Rue el Imam Malik, just off Av Mohammed V behind the post office, Guéliz ☎ 0524 433038, Ⓦ grandcafedelaposte-marrakech.com. Daily 8am–1am. MAP P.73, POCKET MAP B15

More grand than café, this is in fact quite a posh restaurant – France's colonial governor T'hami el Glaoui used to dine here back in the day – serving international cuisine with a menu that changes quite regularly. The menu includes a selection of beef, duck and fish dishes, and main courses mostly go for 125–185dh. For drinks, you can wash it down with a cup of Earl Grey, or there's a choice of rums, tequilas and fine brandies if you prefer something harder.

GRAND CAFÉ DE LA POSTE

## HOTEL FAROUK

66 Av Hassan II, Guéliz ☎ 0524 431989. Daily 11am–9pm. MAP P.73, POCKET MAP B15

From noon the hotel restaurant offers an excellent-value 45–50dh set menu with soup or salad, then couscous, tajine or brochettes, followed by fruit or home-made yoghurt. Alternatively, tuck into one of their excellent wood-oven pizzas (30–40dh).

## KATSURA

1 Rue Oum Errabia, Guéliz ☎ 0524 434358, ⓦ katsura.ma. Daily noon–2.30pm & 7.45–11.30pm. MAP P.73, POCKET MAP D4

Billing itself as a "Thai wok and sushi restaurant", this is Marrakesh's first Thai restaurant, and it's not at all bad, with the usual Thai standards including green or red curries (75–100dh), plus Japanese snacks, mainly sushi (35–50dh), and set menus (100dh lunchtime, 200dh evening). The food's fresh and tasty, and the service is pleasant and efficient. All in all, a nice change from the usual Marrakesh fare.

## LA CRÊPERIE DE MARRAKECH

14 Rue Petit Marché de Guéliz, off Route de Targa, Guéliz ☎ 0524 432208. Mon–Sat noon–3pm & 6–10.30pm. MAP P.73, POCKET MAP A2

Crêpes, naturally – Breton-style ones, apparently – with a choice of sweet or savoury fillings. The latter (40–60dh) include spinach and goat's cheese, or Roquefort, or egg and chorizo. Among the sweet fillings (20–50dh), there's apple with cinnamon, or chestnut cream, or the classic crêpe Suzette (with Grand Marnier liqueur).

## LA TAVERNE

22 Bd Mohammed Zerktouni, Guéliz ☎ 0524 446126. Daily noon–3pm & 7.30–11pm. MAP P.73, POCKET MAP A14

As well as a drinking tavern, this is a pretty decent restaurant – in fact, it claims to be the oldest in town – where you can dine on French and Moroccan food indoors or in a lovely tree-shaded garden. The 130dh set menu isn't bad value either.

## LA TRATTORIA

179 Rue Mohammed el Bekal, Guéliz ☎ 0524 432641, ⓦ latrattoriamarrakech.com. Daily 7.30pm–1am. MAP P.73, POCKET MAP A15

*La Trattoria* serves the best Italian food in town, with impeccable, friendly service and excellent cooking. The restaurant is located in a 1920s house decorated by the acclaimed American designer Bill Willis. As well as freshly made pasta, steaks and escalopes, there's beef medallions in Parmesan – the house speciality – plus a wonderful tiramisu to squeeze in for afters. Expect to pay about 400dh, more with wine.

## LE CANTANZARO

50 Rue Tarik Ben Ziad, Guéliz ☎ 0524 433731. Mon–Sat noon–2.30pm & 7.15–11pm. MAP P.73, POCKET MAP B14

LA CRÊPERIE DE MARRAKECH

This is one of the city's most popular Italian restaurants, crowded at lunchtime and suppertime alike with Marrakshis, expats and tourists. Specialities include *saltimbocca alla romana* and rabbit in mustard sauce, and there's crème brûlée or tiramisu to round it off with. It's licensed but not that expensive (main dishes are 90–115dh, pizzas and pasta 50–70dh). It's always best to book, but you can also just turn up and queue for a table if you don't mind waiting.

### LE DRAGON D'OR

82 Bd Mohammed Zerktouni, Guéliz ☎ 0524 430617. Daily noon–2pm & 7–11pm. MAP P.73, POCKET MAP B14

A pick'n'mix of East Asian cuisine, with bright and cheerful decor, *Le Dragon d'Or* is popular with local families and there's a takeaway service. Dishes include traditional Chinese takeaway favourites (chow mein, sweet and sour and the like), quite a few duck dishes, and a handful of Vietnamese dishes and sushi for good measure. Main dishes are 80–130dh, and there's a 175dh lunchtime set menu. Licensed.

### LE JACARANDA

32 Bd Mohammed Zerktouni, Guéliz ☎ 0524 447215, ⓦ lejacaranda.com. Daily noon–3pm & 7.30–11pm. MAP P.73, POCKET MAP A14

The traditional French cuisine at *Le Jacaranda* is always reliably good. Start perhaps with renowned oysters from Oualidia on the coast (in the form, if you like, of oyster brochettes with smoked duck breast), beef carpaccio, or snails in garlic butter, and follow it with medallions or tournedos of beef, or grilled sea bass flambéed in pastis. À la carte eating will set you back around 350dh a head plus wine; alternatively, there are 100dh and 149dh lunchtime set menus (but only the 149dh menu in the evening).

### L'TCHINE

Ave des Nations Unies at Rue Badr ☎ 0524 438980, ⓦ ltchine-restaurant.com. Daily 7am–11.30pm. MAP P.73, POCKET MAP C4

A good spot to call by for breakfast, lunch or supper, in bright and breezy surrounds, where the food is as slow-cooked and traditional as an Essaouira-style tajine (80dh) or Marrakshi tanjia (120dh), or as fast and modern as a cheese bagel breakfast with yoghurt and OJ (40dh).

### LUNCH D'OR

Rue de l'Imam Ali, Guéliz. Daily 8am–7.30pm. MAP P.73, POCKET MAP D5

It can be hard to find honest-to-goodness cheap Moroccan food in the Ville Nouvelle, but this place is one of a pair opposite the church serving tasty tajines at 25dh a shot, as well as salads, brochettes and pizzas. Great value and very popular with workers on their lunch break.

## MAMA AFRIKA

3 Rue Oum Errabia ☎ 0524 457382. Daily 24hr. MAP P.73, POCKET MAP D4

Done out like a cabaña on some tropical beach, *Mama Afrika* serves coffee, snacks, juices and dishes with an Afro-Caribbean flavour. In fact, they serve everything except alcohol, but there are tasty mocktails, and reggae music to get you in that dancing mood. Main courses 40–55dh.

## RÔTISSERIE DE LA PAIX

68 Rue de Yougoslavie, alongside the former Cinema Lux-Palace, Guéliz ☎ 0524 433118, ⓦwww.restaurant-diaffa.ma/rotisserie. Daily noon–3pm & 7.30pm–midnight. MAP P.73, POCKET MAP B15

An open-air grill, established in 1949, specializing in mixed grills barbecued over wood, usually with a fish option. It's all served either in a salon, which has a roaring fire in winter, or in the shaded garden in summer. Couscous is served on Fridays only. A meal here will set you back around 180dh per head, not including wine.

## THE RED HOUSE

Bd el Yarmouk, opposite the Medina wall, Hivernage ☎ 0524 437040 or 437041, ⓦtheredhouse-marrakech.com. Daily noon–2.30pm & 7.30–10.30pm. MAP P.73, POCKET MAP E6

You'll need to reserve ahead to eat at this palatial riad, which is beautifully decorated in stucco and zellij. There's a Moroccan set menu (370–400dh), featuring pigeon pastilla and lamb tajine with prunes and sesame, or an international menu (same price), all with music and belly-dancing. Desserts include sweet pastilla or apple tart with licorice ice cream. Licensed.

LUNCH D'OR

## WINOO

77 Bd Moulay Rachid (at Rue Mauritania) ☎ 0524 430400. Daily 7am–3am. MAP P.73, POCKET MAP B15

A justifiably popular café-restaurant where you can stop by for a juice or a smoothie (the avocado and almond is especially delicious), a huge salad or a tasty tajine (the usual options, but also things like shrimp), all freshly made, well presented and very inexpensive (a meal won't cost much more than 50dh). It gets very busy at mealtimes but that isn't exactly surprising.

# Bars

## AFRICAN CHIC

5 Rue Oum Errabia, Guéliz. ☎ 0524 431424, ⓦafrican-chic.com. Daily 8pm–4am. MAP P.73, POCKET MAP D4

One of Marrakesh's most congenial bars, *African Chic* is informal and relaxed, with cocktails, wines, beers, tapas (five for 70dh, eight for 100dh), salads, pasta, and meat and fish dishes. Live Latin and Gnaoua music every night from 10pm.

## CAFÉ ATLAS

Place Abdelmoumen Ben Ali, Guéliz
☎ 0524 448888. Daily 10am–11pm. MAP P.73,
POCKET MAP A14

A pavement café in the very centre of Guéliz, but wander inside, and hey presto, it is magically transformed into a bar, with bottled beer, spirits and plates of bar snacks on the counter. In theory, you could take your drink out on the pavement, but that would be considered rather indiscreet, so it's best to remain within, where respectable passers-by won't notice that you're indulging in alcohol.

## CHESTERFIELD PUB

Hotel Nassim, 119 Av Mohammed V, Guéliz
☎ 0524 446401. Tues, Wed, Fri & Sat
11am–1am, Sun, Mon & Thurs 3pm–1am.
MAP P.73, POCKET MAP B14

Upstairs in the *Hotel Nassim*, this supposedly English-style pub is one of Marrakesh's more sophisticated watering holes, with a cosy if rather smoky bar area, all soft seats and muted lighting. There's also a more relaxed, open-air poolside terrace on which to lounge with your draught beer or cocktail of a summer evening.

## IBIS MOUSSAFIR HOTEL

Av Hassan II, by the old train station entrance, Guéliz ☎ 0524 435936. Daily 24hr.
MAP P.73, POCKET MAP A4

This hotel bar is not the most atmospheric bar in town – just an area of the lobby, it has no feeling of intimacy at all. Nonetheless, it has the advantage of being a place where women can feel comfortable having a quiet drink or two.

## KECHMARA

3 Rue de la Liberté, Guéliz ☎ 0524 422532,
🌐 kechmara.com. Mon–Sat 10am–1am.
MAP P.73, POCKET MAP B15

Downstairs, *Kechmara* is a cool bar-café with a slightly Japanese feel; upstairs there's an open-air terrace with a contemporary design. A hip place to hang out, with modern art exhibitions and live music (soul, jazz and funk) on the terrace (Wed & Fri evenings from 8.30pm), it also serves food including burgers (110dh), fish and chips (100dh) and, from 6.30pm nightly, tapas.

## L'ESCALE

Rue Mauritanie, just off Av Mohammed V,
Guéliz ☎ 0524 433447. Daily 9am–11pm.
MAP P.73, POCKET MAP B15

A down-at-heel, spit-and-sawdust kind of bar, this place has been going since 1947 and specializes in good bar snacks, such as fried fish or spicy merguez sausages – you could even come here for lunch or dinner (there's a dining area at the back). The interior isn't recommended for unaccompanied women, especially in the evening, but there's family-friendly (no booze) terrace eating out front by day.

KECHMARA

### SAMOVAR

145 Rue Mohammed el Bekal, Guéliz, next to the *Hotel Oudaya*, Guéliz. Daily 8am–10pm. MAP P.73, POCKET MAP A14

*Samovar* is an old-school, low-life drinking den; a male hangout with bar girls in attendance. The customers get more and more out of it as the evening progresses – if you want to see the underbelly of Morocco's drinking culture, this is the place. Definitely not recommended for women visitors, however.

### SKY BAR

*Renaissance Hotel*, Place Abdelmoumen Ben Ali, Guéliz ☎ 0524 337777. Daily 10pm–1am. MAP P.73, POCKET MAP A14

Colonial-era building regulations in Marrakesh help keep the city's skyline down to five stories, but somehow the *Renaissance Hotel*, smack-bang in the middle of downtown Guéliz escaped the limitation and its 7th-floor rooftop bar thus has absolutely the best view in town. Although a beer here will cost you 60dh, the bar's terrace is absolutely Marrakesh's top spot to sip one while watching the sun set.

# Nightclubs

### DIAMANT NOIR

Rue Oum Errabia, behind *Hôtel Marrakesh* ☎ 0524 446391. Daily 10pm–4am. MAP P.73, POCKET MAP B15

Un-hip, un-trendy and unpretentious, this cheap-rate disco is a place to let your hair down rather than show off your clothes or "see and be seen". The beautiful people may look down their noses at it, but it's at least as much fun as whichever of the posher clubs are "in" this season. Western pop and disco alternate with North African

and Middle Eastern sounds, and there's a decent range of drinks, a mainly young crowd, and a (discreetly) gay contingent. You don't have to dress up like a dog's dinner to get in, trainers are fine and entry is free – you just pay for drinks.

### MONTECRISTO

20 Rue Ibn Aïcha, Guéliz ☎ 0524 439031, ⓦ montecristomarrakech.com. Daily 8pm–4am. Free entry. MAP P.73, POCKET MAP B2

Four spaces in one venue: a stylishly decorated restaurant serving decent if not outstanding food; a pub with live music from 11pm and a Cuban theme including (naturally) Montecristo cigars; a nightclub with DJs playing Arabic and Western dance sounds; and a rooftop *"Sky Bar"*, where you can puff on *sheesha* pipes or Havana cigars while belly-dancers disport themselves for your entertainment. Hookers work the bar, European tourists being their main punters, but aside from that it's quite a posh joint, and the smoking terrace is an excellent chill-out zone for the nightclub.

PACHA MARRAKECH

## PACHA MARRAKECH

Av Mohammed VI (southern extension),
Nouvelle Zone Hôtelière de l'Aguedal ☎ 0524
388400, ⓦ pachamarrakech.com. Bar Tues–Sun
7pm–1am; Club Thurs–Sun midnight–4am.
Entry 150dh Thurs & Fri, 200dh Sat, more for
special events. MAP P.73, POCKET MAP D9

The Marrakesh branch of the
famous Ibiza club, now an
international chain, claims to
have the biggest and best sound
system in Africa, and it's
certainly the place to come if
DJing skills, acoustics and
visuals are important to your
clubbing experience. Big-name
DJs from abroad regularly play
here – check the website for
current line-ups. It also has two
restaurants (one European, one
Moroccan), a chill-out zone
and a swimming pool.

## SO NIGHT LOUNGE

Sofitel Marrakesh, Rue Haroun Errachid,
Hivernage ☎ 0656 515009. Daily 7pm–4am.
Entry 250dh. MAP P.73, POCKET MAP D6

This lounge bar, restaurant and
nightclub combo has quickly
become one of the trendiest
venues in town, catering to an
extremely well-coiffed, jet-set
crowd. You'll find everyone
from the Marrakchi elite to
weekending yacht owners in
from the Riviera. Regular live
acts (until 1am) play
everything from rock to raï
– the French-based group
Alabina, for example – after
which the dancefloor opens up
to the sounds of house and dub
DJs. Dress to impress or you
won't get in.

## THEATRO

Hotel es Saadi, Av el Kadissia (also spelt
Qadassia), Hivernage ☎ 0524 448811,
ⓦ theatromarrakech.com. Daily
11.30pm–4am. Entry 180–500dh, depending
on what's on. MAP P.73, POCKET MAP D6

One of Marrakesh's more
interesting nightclubs, located
in, as its name suggests, an old

SO NIGHT LOUNGE

theatre. Nights are themed
(ladies' night on Tues, for
example, and hip-hop night on
Thurs) and the atmosphere is
sophisticated – though make no
mistake, by the early hours the
crowd are really going for it.
Music is the usual mix of house,
trance, techno and RnB with
Algerian raï and Middle Eastern
pop, but the special effects and
circus-style performers on stage
make it a cut above most
Marrakesh clubs.

## VIP CLUB

Place de la Liberté, Guéliz. Daily bar
8pm–4am; club midnight–4am ☎ 0661
152026. Entry 200dh. MAP P.73, POCKET MAP D5

Stairs lead down from the
entrance to the first level,
where there's a lounge bar, with
happy hour until 11pm, and
then (from midnight) further
down to the deepest level,
where there's what the French
call a boîte, meaning a sweaty
little nightclub. It's got a
circular dancefloor and a small
bar area, but despite its diminu-
tive size, the place rarely seems
to be full.

# Atlas excursions

The countryside around Marrakesh is some of the most beautiful in Morocco. The High Atlas mountains that make such a spectacular backdrop to the city are even more impressive when you're actually among them. For a spot of hiking, or even skiing, they're easy enough to reach in an hour or two by *grand taxi*, usually from Place Youssef Tachfine (Sidi Mimoun), south of the Koutoubia. Imlil is the best base for mountain treks, but Setti Fatma, in the beautiful Ourika Valley, is more picturesque, and handier for less strenuous walking, while Oukaïmeden is Morocco's premier ski resort.

## IMLIL AND AROUND

MAP P.89

You can take in the village of **Imlil** on a day-trip out of Marrakesh, 65km away, but it's more worthwhile if you spend a night or two there and do a bit of walking in the surrounding countryside. There's little to the village itself, which came into existence purely as a trekking base, and the only real sight, aside from the mountain scenery, is the *Kasbah du Toubkal*, formerly the palace of the local *caid* (chieftain), now a hotel and restaurant (see p.115 & p.91). To reach Imlil by public transport, get a shared *grand taxi* from Place Youssef Tachfine to **Asni** (1hr, 20dh), where there are *grands taxis* on to Imlil (30min, 10dh). Occasionally there are taxis all the way for 30dh a place. Alternatively, you could charter a *grand taxi* to take you up there from Marrakesh, which should work out at 400–450dh for the round trip, including three or four hours' waiting time.

From Imlil the mule trail back down to Asni is a

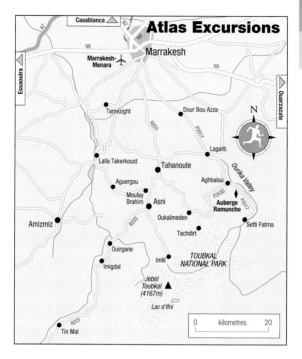

relatively easy six-hour **hike**, and there are vehicles from Asni back to Marrakesh until around 5pm. Alternatively, you could just have **lunch** in Imlil and then head back into town by taxi.

You could also take on the short trek from Imlil to **Tachdirt** (3–4hr), which has a *refuge* (basic hostel) run by the Club Alpin Français where

you can spend the night. From Tachdirt, it's a day's trek down to **Setti Fatma** (see p.90), where there's transport back to Marrakesh.

With the right equipment, clothing and supplies, it's even possible to climb **Jebel Toubkal** (4167m), North Africa's highest peak, though this is not an ascent to be taken lightly.

## Trekking and hiking in the Atlas

You could spend many days trekking in the High Atlas, but there are also trails to suit the casual hiker and routes that can be covered in a day. The easiest walks take in pretty valleys spread with a patchwork of little fields dotted with walnut trees.

To hire a **guide** (expect to pay around 500dh per day), contact the offices (called *Bureau de Guides et Accompagnateurs en Montagne*) in either Imlil (☎ 0524 485626, ⊕ bureaudesguidesimlil.com) or Setti Fatma (☎ 0673 520907, ✉ meltsan2000@yahoo.fr). In Marrakesh, the *Hotel Ali* (see p.104) is one of the best places to get **information** and arrange guides.

## SETTI FATMA AND THE OURIKA VALLEY

MAP P.89

At the top of the highly scenic **Ourika Valley**, with high mountains and terraced fields on both sides, the village of **Setti Fatma**, 67km out of Marrakesh, is more picturesque than Imlil, and more worthwhile for a day-trip. The easiest way to get there is to take a shared *grand taxi* from the southern end of Rue Ibn Rachid (or a #25 bus from Place Youssef Tachfine) to **Lagarb**, where there are shared *grands taxis* on to Setti Fatma. You may even find a direct shared taxi from Rue Ibn Rachid (around 1hr; 25dh per person), or you can charter a whole taxi (400–450dh for the round trip plus waiting time).

Setti Fatma is an excellent base for scenic **walks**, with six (sometimes seven) waterfalls above the village, the first of which can be reached very easily; you'll have no shortage of would-be guides offering to show you the way for a tip (of course), best agreed in advance. The walk to all seven falls and back takes around two and a half hours.

## OUKAÏMEDEN

MAP P.89

The High Atlas village of **Oukaïmeden** ("Ouka" for short), 74km from Marrakesh, has five ski lifts and 20km of

WATERFALLS AT SETTI FATMA

runs. There are nursery and intermediate runs on the lower slopes for the less advanced, and off-piste skiing and snowboarding are also available.

To get from Marrakesh to Oukaïmeden, you can charter a *grand taxi* for a day-trip (expect to pay 600dh there and back), or else get to Lagarb (see above), where there are minibuses to Oukaïmeden in season (Dec–April); coming back, try to leave by 3 or 4pm to be sure of transport connections.

**Ski lift passes** cost 50–100dh per day, and lessons are available from local instructors. You can rent **equipment** from shops near the hotel *Chez Juju* (see p.116) and at the bottom of the slope for around 100dh a day; snowboards and toboggans are also available.

## Setti Fatma Moussem

Every year in mid-August, Setti Fatma holds a **moussem** dedicated to the local saint after whom the village is named. The saint's tomb stands by the river on the way to the waterfalls above the village. Although the *moussem* is religious in origin, it is just as much a fair and market, attracting Sufi mystics as well as performers like those of Marrakesh's Jemaa el Fna.

# Restaurants: Imlil

### CAFÉ ATLAS TOUBKAL

300m up from the taxi stand and across the river ☎ 0676 047545. Daily 8am–11pm.

Perched on a rock with a rooftop terrace giving a vista over the village, this is a great place for a morning coffee, and also pretty good for a tajine (80dh) at lunchtime.

### CAFÉ DU SOLEIL

By the taxi stand ☎ 0524 485622, ⓦ hotelsoleilimlil.com. Daily 8am–9pm.

Cheap little restaurant attached to the *Hotel Soleil*. Nothing fancy, but they'll do you a decent tajine for 50–60dh.

### CAFÉ LES AMIS

200m up the road from the taxi stand. Daily around noon–7pm.

Cheap and cheerful diner, which can lay on tajine for one, two or more if ordered at least an hour and a half in advance.

### KASBAH DU TOUBKAL

☎ 0524 485611, ⓦ kasbahdutoubkal.com. Daily noon–3pm & 7–9.30pm.

This British-run hotel (see p.115) offers an excellent €30–35 (312–365dh) set menu, which should be booked at least a day in advance. In fact, the *Kasbah* can even organize the whole day-trip from Marrakesh as a package, at €85 (885dh) per person (minimum two). At the very least, it's worth popping in for a mint tea on their scenic terrace. Unlicensed, but you can bring your own alcohol.

# Restaurants: Ourika Valley

### HOTEL-RESTAURANT ASGAOUR

Setti Fatma, 300m below the taxi stand ☎ 0524 485294. Daily 7am–11pm.

One of the better choices among Setti Fatma's hotel restaurants, the *Asgaour* serves an excellent-value 50–55dh set menu based on tajine as the main course.

### HOTEL SETTI FATMA

Setti Fatma, 350m below the taxi stand ☎ 0666 454972. Daily 7.30am–4pm.

The restaurant at this hotel (see p.116) is set in a garden overlooking the river, which makes it a lovely location for a meal. The set menu of salad, tagine and tea is 60dh.

### RESTAURANT DES CASCADES

Setti Fatma ☎ 0670 173083. Daily 6am–8pm.

One of a group of small restaurants just across the river from the village (on a very rickety bridge), *Les Cascades* has a series of scenic terraces and is a great place to stop for a mint tea, with 60dh tajines also available.

### RESTAURANT LE NOYER

Setti Fatma, 100m below the taxi stand ☎ 0661 596846. Daily 11am–6pm.

This restaurant with a riverside terrace offers a small selection of tasty tajines, brochettes and salads, with a choice of set menus (100–150dh).

KASBAH DU TOUBKAL

# Essaouira

Tourists have had a special relationship with the seaside resort of Essaouira, around 170km west of Marrakesh, since the 1960s, when its popularity as a hippy resort attracted the likes of Jimi Hendrix and Frank Zappa. Since then it has become a centre for artists and windsurfers, but despite increasing numbers of foreign visitors it remains one of the most laid-back and likeable towns in Morocco. The whitewashed and blue-shuttered houses of its Medina, enclosed by spectacular ramparts, provide a colourful backdrop to a long, sandy beach, and whether you're here for the sport, the art or just the sand, you're sure to fall under its spell.

## THE MEDINA

MAP P.94–95

The fairy-tale **ramparts** around Essaouira's Medina may look medieval, but they actually date from the reign of eighteenth-century sultan Sidi Mohammed Ben Abdallah, who commissioned a French military architect named Theodore Cornut to build a new town on a site previously occupied by a series of forts. The result is a walled medina that blends Moroccan and French layouts, combining a crisscross of main streets with a labyrinth of alleyways between them.

At the heart of the Medina are the main **souks**, centred on two arcades either side of Rue Mohammed Zerktouni. On the northwest side is the **spice souk**, where culinary aromatics join incense, traditional cosmetics and even natural aphrodisiacs billed as "herbal Viagra". Across the way, the **jewellers' souk** sells not just gems but also all kinds of crafts.

The western part of the Medina, the **Kasbah**, centres on **Place Prince Moulay el Hassan**. This is the town's main square, where locals and tourists alike linger over a mint

ESSAOUIRA RAMPARTS

tea or a coffee and enjoy the lazy pace of life. The square to the south, the **Mechouar**, is bounded by an imposing wall topped by a clocktower and flanked by palm trees, in whose shade townspeople often take a breather from the heat of the day.

### THE NORTH BASTION

Rue de la Skala. Daily sunrise–sunset. Free. MAP P.94–95

The city's **north bastion** commands panoramic views across the Medina and out to sea. It was one of the main

Essaouira locations used in Orson Welles's 1952 screen version of *Othello*. Along the top is a collection of European **cannons**, presented to Sidi Mohammed Ben Abdallah by ambitious nineteenth-century merchants.

Down below, built into the ramparts along the Rue de la Skala, you can see some of the town's many **marquetry** and **woodcarving** workshops, where artisans produce amazingly painstaking and beautiful pieces from **thuya** wood.

## Getting to Essaouira

Reaching Essaouira from Marrakesh by public transport is a cinch, though the journey time means you'll probably want to stay overnight. The cheapest way is to get a **bus** (18 daily; 3hr 30min; around 60dh) from the *gare routière* (see p.120). You arrive at Essaouira's *gare routière*, a ten-minute walk outside the town's Bab Doukkala, or a short *petit taxi* ride from the central Bab es Sebaa (7dh). A faster and more comfortable bus service is provided by **Supratours** (6 daily; 3hr; 70–100dh), leaving from their office in Marrakesh near the train station and arriving at Essaouira's Bab Marrakesh. **CTM**, the state bus company, also run two daily buses to Essaouira from the *gare routière* or from their office on Rue Abou Bakr Seddik (75dh). Finally, there are shared **grands taxis** to Essaouira (2hr 30min; 100dh) from the rank behind Marrakesh's *gare routière*; in Essaouira they might drop you in town itself, though they actually operate from a yard by the *gare routière*.

Essaouira's **airport**, 15km south of town, with no public transport (taxi 200dh for up to six) has flights to Luton with EasyJet. Essaouira's **tourist office** is located on Avenue du Caire (Mon–Fri 9am–4pm; ☎ 0524 783532).

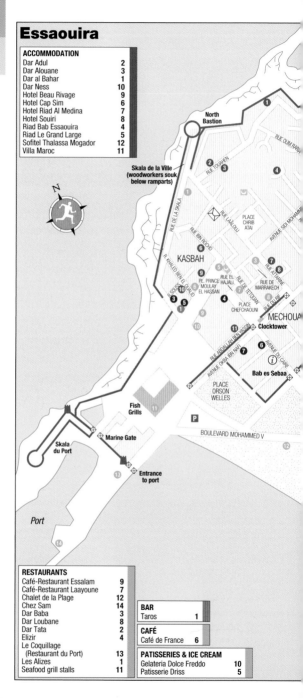

# Essaouira

**ACCOMMODATION**

| | |
|---|---|
| Dar Adul | 2 |
| Dar Alouane | 3 |
| Dar al Bahar | 1 |
| Dar Ness | 10 |
| Hotel Beau Rivage | 9 |
| Hotel Cap Sim | 6 |
| Hotel Riad Al Medina | 7 |
| Hotel Souiri | 8 |
| Riad Bab Essaouira | 4 |
| Riad Le Grand Large | 5 |
| Sofitel Thalassa Mogador | 12 |
| Villa Maroc | 11 |

North Bastion

RUE OUM BABA

RUE TOUAHEN

Skala de la Ville
(woodworkers souk
below ramparts)

N

RUE DE LA SKALA

RUE IBN ROCHD

RUE LAALOU

PLACE CHRIB ATAI

AVENUE SIDI MOHAMMED

KASBAH

R. KHALED BEN EL OUALID

RUE EL HAJALI

Pl. PRINCE MOULAY EL HASSAN

RUE DE MARRAKECH

RUE DE TETOUAN

RUE ATTARINE

RUE OUDE

PLACE CHEFCHAOUNI

MECHOUA

Clocktower

RUE ABDALLAH BEN YASSINE

AVENUE OKBA BEN NAFI

AVENUE DU CAIRE

(i)

Bab es Sebaa

PLACE ORSON WELLES

Fish Grills

P

BOULEVARD MOHAMMED V

Marine Gate

Skala du Port

Entrance to port

Port

**RESTAURANTS**

| | |
|---|---|
| Café-Restaurant Essalam | 9 |
| Café-Restaurant Laayoune | 7 |
| Chalet de la Plage | 12 |
| Chez Sam | 14 |
| Dar Baba | 3 |
| Dar Loubane | 8 |
| Dar Tata | 2 |
| Elizir | 4 |
| Le Coquillage (Restaurant du Port) | 13 |
| Les Alizes | 1 |
| Seafood grill stalls | 11 |

**BAR**

| | |
|---|---|
| Taros | 1 |

**CAFÉ**

| | |
|---|---|
| Café de France | 6 |

**PATISSERIES & ICE CREAM**

| | |
|---|---|
| Gelateria Dolce Freddo | 10 |
| Patisserie Driss | 5 |

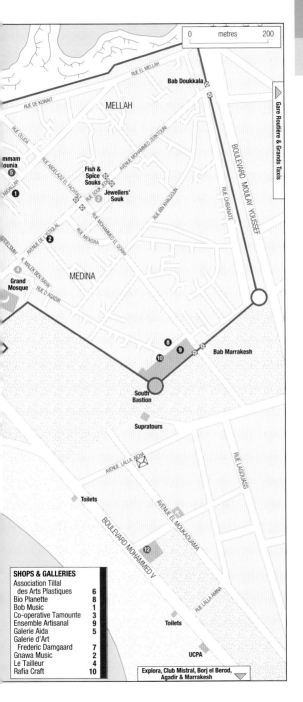

0  metres  200

Gare Routière & Grands Taxis

RUE EL MELLAH

**Bab Doukkala**

RUE DE KUWAIT

MELLAH

RUE OUDA

RUE ABDELAZIZ EL FICHTALI

AVENUE MOHAMMED ZERKTOUNI

mmam
ounia
**⑤**

ABDALLAH

**①**

**Fish &
Spice
Souks**

RUE SOUK JDID

**Jewellers'
Souk**

**②**

RUE BEN KHALDOUN

BOULEVARD MOULAY YOUSSEF

RUE CHENATE

RUE ABDELSMIH

AVENUE DE L'ISTIQLAL

**②**

RUE MENSRA

RUE MOHAMMED EL OORRY

ABDELSMIH

R. MALEK BEN RAHAL

MEDINA

**Grand
Mosque**

RUE O AGADIR

**④**

RUE ABDELSMIH

**⑧**

**⑩**

**⑨**

**Bab Marrakesh**

**South
Bastion**

**Supratours**

AVENUE LALLA AICHA

RUE LAGOUASS

**Toilets**

AVENUE EL MOUKAOUAMA

BOULEVARD MOHAMMED V

**⑫**

RUE LALLA AMINA

**Toilets**

**UCPA**

**Explora, Club Mistral, Borj el Berod,
Agadir & Marrakesh**

**SHOPS & GALLERIES**

| | |
|---|---|
| Association Tillal des Arts Plastiques | 6 |
| Bio Planette | 8 |
| Bob Music | 1 |
| Co-operative Tamounte | 3 |
| Ensemble Artisanal | 9 |
| Galerie Aida | 5 |
| Galerie d'Art Frederic Damgaard | 7 |
| Gnawa Music | 2 |
| Le Tailleur | 4 |
| Rafia Craft | 10 |

## The Gnaoua Festival

Essaouira's main annual event is the **Gnaoua and World Music Festival** (ⓦfestival-gnaoua.net), held in May or June. The festival focuses chiefly on the music of the Gnaoua, a Moroccan Sufi brotherhood with West African roots going back to the days of slavery. Stages are set up in the plaza between Place Prince Moulay el Hassan and the port, and outside Bab Marrakesh, and performers come from Morocco, Europe and West Africa. During the festival, you can expect hotels and transport to be full, so book well ahead if possible.

### THE SKALA DU PORT

Daily 9am–5pm. 10dh. MAP P.94–95

The **Skala du Port**, the square sea bastion by the harbour, is topped by lookout posts in each of its four corners and is worth popping into for the **views** from the ramparts. Looking east, you have a brilliant vista along the seaward side of the walled city. To the south, the Skala overlooks the bustling **port area**, where local wooden fishing boats are built or repaired, and where the fishing fleet brings in the day's catch.

### THE BEACH

MAP P.94–95

The main **beach**, to the south of town, extends for miles. On

CAMEL ON ESSAOUIRA BEACH

its closest stretches, the chief activity is **football** – a game is virtually always in progress, and at weekends there's a full-scale local league.

The wind here can be a bit remorseless for sunbathing in spring and summer, but it's perfect for **windsurfing**, and Essaouira is Morocco's number-one windsurfing resort. Surfing, windsurfing and kitesurfing equipment can be rented on the beach at UCPA (ⓣ0524 474354, ⓦucpamaroc.com), 500m south of the Medina, where you can also arrange to have lessons. Equipment and lessons are also available 1km down the beach at Explora (ⓣ0611 475188, ⓦexploramorocco.com) or Club Mistral (ⓣ0524 783934, ⓦoceanvagabond.com). The water is cool enough to make a wetsuit essential year-round.

If you head further along the beach, you'll pass the riverbed of the Oued Ksob (which can't be crossed at high tide) and come upon the ruins of an eighteenth-century circular fort, the **Borj el Berod**, which looks as though it is almost melting into the sand. The story that it inspired Jimi Hendrix's "Castles Made of Sand" is definitely apocryphal, though, as the track was recorded before Hendrix came to Morocco.

# Shops and galleries

## ASSOCIATION TILLAL DES ARTS PLASTIQUES

4 Av du Caire ☎ 0524 475424. Mon–Sat 9am–12.30pm & 3–7pm. MAP P.94–95

Essaouira's cheap and cheerful art gallery, where you can pick up small and affordable works of art by the fifty painters who make up this excellent local cooperative, including Najia Keirairate's colourful naive domestic scenes, and Hamid Bouhali's humorous caricatures of Moroccan life, for as little as 200dh.

## BIO PLANETTE

101bis Rue d'Agadir ☎ 0661 395657. Mon–Sat 9am–5.30pm. MAP P.94–95

The floor of this shop is covered with the shells of argan nuts, whose kernels are hulled and crushed (in the shop itself) to extract a much prized nutty oil, which you can buy for cooking (from toasted argan nuts) or for cosmetic use (from raw nuts), along with a wide range of organic culinary and medicinal spices including locally grown cumin, which unfortunately they sell only ready ground. The proprietor is usually on hand to explain all the various spices and their properties.

## BOB MUSIC

4 Rue Youssef Ben Tachfine ☎ 0668 252695. Daily 9am–8pm. MAP P.94–95

Named after Bob Marley, this musical instrument shop sells several types of Moroccan drums, Gnaoua castanets, lutes, *ginbris* (an instrument not unlike a lute, but rather more rustic), and even the sort of pipes used by snake charmers.

## CO-OPERATIVE TAMOUNTE

6 Rue Souss ☎ 0524 785611. Daily 9am–7pm. MAP P.94–95

This is a good place to buy both thuya marquetry and argan oil. In both cases it comes from cooperative enterprises – a co-op of fifteen artisans makes the thuya products, and a rural women's co-op makes the oil. Also in both cases, the quality is good and the prices are fixed, marked, and comparatively low, so you're not only contributing to fair-trade democratic enterprise, but also getting a good deal while you're at it.

## ENSEMBLE ARTISANAL

Rue Mohammed el Qorry, just inside Bab Marrakesh. Daily 8am–6pm. MAP P.95

This bright, whitewashed courtyard hosts a handful of thuya carvers, an artisan jeweller – Mohammed Bizbiz, trained in Arab, Berber and Jewish styles – and the Association Création Mogador, a group of six local artists whose gallery is at the far end on the left. In a courtyard on the right, a Brazilian ombú tree, one of only three in Morocco, was planted when the town was founded in the eighteenth century.

BOB MUSIC

## GALERIE AIDA

2 Rue de la Skala ☎ 0524 476290. Daily 1–8pm. MAP P.94-95

Owned by a New Yorker, this shop starts off at the front selling secondhand books, mainly in English and at rather high prices, but as you head deeper inside, there's all kinds of interesting, superior bric-a-brac. Prices are still high, but at least you know you aren't getting sold any *trafika* (phoney antiques, unfortunately rather common in Essaouira's art and antique shops).

## GALERIE D'ART FREDERIC DAMGAARD

Av Okba Ibn Nafi, Mechouar ☎ 0524 784446. Daily 9am–1pm & 3–7pm. MAP P.94-95

Essaouira's artists have made a name for themselves in both Morocco and Europe. Those whose paintings and sculptures are exhibited here in Essaouira's top gallery have developed their own highly distinctive styles, in some cases attracting an entourage of imitators. The gallery, and its atelier at 2 Rue El Hijalli, just off Place Chefchouni, were founded by a Danish furniture designer, and are now run by two Belgian art lovers, hand-picked by Damgaard to succeed him.

## GNAWA MUSIC

60 Av de l'Istiqlal ☎ 0604 375317. Daily 10am–10pm. MAP P.94-95

This shop sells CDs (50dh) and cassettes (15dh) of North African and Muslim West African music – most especially music of the type played at the annual Gnaoua Festival (see box, p.96), of which a compilation album is released each year. There's also classical Moroccan, Arab-Andalusian, Moroccan folk and Algerian *raï*. Mogador Music a few doors down at no. 52 sells a selection focusing more on *raï*, pop and foreign sounds.

## LE TAILLEUR

3 Rue de la el Hajali ☎ 0618 502440. Daily 9am–7pm. MAP P.94-95

A tailor, as the name says, but one who makes light cotton and linen clothing, mostly in cream, white, black and grey: beautifully cool in Morocco's sometimes relentless heat. Shirts, drawstring-trousers, dresses and kaftans start at 130dh. They also nowadays sell clothes made of the same fabrics, but in brighter colours.

## RAFIA CRAFT

82 Rue d'Agadir ☎ 0524 783632. Mon–Sat 10am–1pm & 3–7pm. MAP P.94-95

A little-known local craft in Essaouira is the use of raffia (a straw-like fibre made from palm leaves) to make clothes, handbags, and above all, in this shop, shoes. All the items on sale here are the creations of local designer Miro Abihssira, and go for fixed prices, which are displayed at the counter. A pair of mocassins will set you back around 450dh for women's, 500dh for men's.

GALERIE D'ART FREDERIC DAMGAARD

# Café

## CAFÉ DE FRANCE

Pl Prince Moulay el Hassan. Daily
6.30am–10.30pm. MAP P.94–95

There's a feeling of faded French
imperialism to this 1917 colonial
café, still at the heart of
Essaouira street life a century
on. In the cavernous blue-and-
white interior, Souiris (the locals,
that is) check their betting slips
over a *nuss-nuss* (coffee
half-and-half with milk) while
the tourists take their seats
outside on the square – Essaouira's top people-watching spot by
far. The food's worth avoiding
here, but the coffee and the mint
tea are both excellent, and you
couldn't hope for a better
location to linger over them.

# Patisseries and ice cream

## GELATERIA DOLCE FREDDO

On the plaza between Pl Prince Moulay el
Hassan and the port. Daily 8am–10pm.
MAP P.94–95

Delicious Italian ice creams at
just 15dh for a small
(two-scoop) cup or cone to take
away, or 20dh for a bowl to eat
on the square. The tiramisu
flavour is heavenly, the hazelnut
isn't bad either, and other
flavours include forest fruits,
cherry ripple and lemon sorbet.

## PATISSERIE DRISS

10 Rue el Hajali, just off Pl Prince Moulay el
Hassan ☎ 0524 475793. Daily 7am–9pm. MAP
P.94–95

Serving delicious fresh pastries
and coffee in a quiet leafy
courtyard, this place is well
established as one of Essaouira's
most popular meeting places.
It's the ideal spot for a leisurely

GELATERIA DOLCE FREDDO

breakfast (set breakfasts
21–30dh), or you can, of
course, buy pastries to go.

# Restaurants

## CAFÉ-RESTAURANT ESSALAM

23 Pl Prince Moulay el Hassan. Daily
9am–4pm & 7–10pm. MAP P.94–95

*Essalam* has some of the
cheapest set menus in town
(30–65dh), and certainly offers
value for money, though the
choice is a little bit limited. On
the walls you will see small
watercolours by Brittany-born
Charles Kérival, who often
visits and paints in Essaouira.

## CAFÉ-RESTAURANT LAAYOUNE

4 Rue el Hajali ☎ 0524 474643. Daily noon–3pm
& 7–10.30pm, Fri noon–3pm. MAP P.94–95

*Laayoune* is good for
moderately priced tajines and
other Moroccan staples in a
relaxed setting with friendly
service, plush orange cushions
to sit on, candlelit tables and a
menu in English on request.
You can eat à la carte (main
dishes around 70dh) or choose
from a range of tajine- and
couscous-based set menus
(78–98dh).

## CHALET DE LA PLAGE

Bd Mohammed V, on the seafront, just above the high-tide mark ☎ 0524 475972. Daily noon–2.30pm & 6.30–10pm. MAP P.94–95

Originally built of wood by the Ferraud family in 1924, the *Chalet de la Plage* building, barnacled with marine mementos, is now a little gloomy, but the seafood and sea views remain truly memorable. Specialities include sea bass steak, oyster tajine and stuffed squid. Avoid lunchtime when day-trippers overwhelm the place. Licensed, with 180dh set menus.

## CHEZ SAM

In the fishing port ☎ 0661 157485. Daily noon–3pm & 7–10.30pm. MAP P.94–95

An Essaouira institution – a wooden shack, built like a boat, set seductively right by the waterfront in the harbour. Service can be a bit hit-and-miss but the portions are generous, the fish is usually cooked pretty well, and you can watch the fishing boats through the portholes. The best fish is only available à la carte (main dishes around 80–120dh);

there's a good-value set menu for 120dh, or one with lobster for 250dh. Licensed.

## DAR BABA

2 Rue de Marrakech ☎ 0524 476809. Daily except Wed 12.30–2.30pm & 6.30–9.30pm. MAP P.94–95

This upstairs restaurant has a short but sweet menu of Italian dishes, including mixed antipasti, fish soup and (for dessert) sorbet. It's most celebrated for its own fresh pasta, though (55–75dh). Licensed.

## DAR LOUBANE

24 Rue du Rif, near Pl Chefchaouni ☎ 0524 476296. Daily noon–3pm & 6–11pm. MAP P.94–95

On the ground-floor patio of an attractive eighteenth-century mansion, this upmarket restaurant serves up fine Moroccan and French cuisine (main dishes around 55–120dh, lunchtime set menu 100–150dh) among an eccentric collection of interesting, sometimes rather kitsch odds and ends that decorate the walls and the courtyard. There's live Gnaoua music on Saturday evening, when it's advisable to make a booking. Licensed.

## DAR TATA

In the grain souk ☎ 0661 774676. Daily 9.30am–6.30pm or later. MAP P.95

A lovely little budget restaurant, slap-bang in the middle of the Medina. Ignore the 85dh meat set menu and go instead for the 95dh fish one, starting with a delicious fish soup, followed by whatever's good from the day's catch, all beautifully presented and served with a smile.

## ELIZIR

1 Rue d'Agadir ☎ 0524 472103. Daily 7.30–11pm. MAP P.94–95

This pioneering little restaurant boasts eclectic retro decor and

GNAOUA DANCER AT DAR LOUBANE

GRILLED SARDINES, ESSAOUIRA STYLE

a harmonious fusion of Italian and Moroccan cuisine using locally sourced ingredients. Dishes change regularly but typically include inky black cuttlefish risotto, ricotta ravioli with basil and pistachio and organic chicken tajine with figs and gorgonzola. Main courses go for 130–160dh. Wine available.

### LE COQUILLAGE (RESTAURANT DU PORT)

In the fishing port ☎ 0524 784737. Daily 12.30–10pm. MAP P.94–95
This competitor to the older *Chez Sam* is set in an imposing stone building on the quayside with a seashell-encrusted entrance. On offer are à la carte fish and shellfish or a choice of seafood set menus at 120dh (three courses with sole or mullet), 160dh (four courses) or 250dh (four courses with lobster or crawfish). Licensed.

### LES ALIZES

28 Rue de la Skala ☎ 0524 476819. Daily noon–3pm & 7–10pm. MAP P.94–95
This little place away from the mainstream has built itself quite a reputation for well-prepared traditional Moroccan dishes. Choice is limited to an 129dh set menu, but everything is absolutely delicious. Wine is available; booking advised.

### SEAFOOD GRILL STALLS

Off Pl Prince Moulay el Hassan, on the way to the port. Daily noon–10pm. MAP P.94–95
An absolute must if you're staying in Essaouira is a meal at one of these makeshift grill stalls, with wooden tables and benches. Each displays a selection of freshly caught fish, prawns, squid, lobster and other seafood delights – all you need to do is check the price (posted up on a board at either end) and select the marine denizens of your choice, which are whisked off to the barbecue to reappear on your plate a few minutes later. Unfortunately, some of the stalls hustle shamelessly for business and (usually the same ones) may overcharge or pull stunts such as choosing you the most expensive fish – best policy is to avoid those that try to accost you. A menu of mixed fish with salad will set you back 60dh, a lobster or langouste supper about 150dh.

# Bar

## TAROS

Pl Moulay Hassan (entrance in Rue de la Skala) ☎ 0524 476407, ⊕ taroscafe.com. Daily 9am–1am. MAP P.94–95
It's fun, fun, fun at this jolly rooftop bar with palm parasols and patio furniture, live music and even a house magician. It's the perfect spot to enjoy a beer or a cocktail around dusk, and the food's pretty good too, with dishes like fish and courgette lasagne, squid tajine or crab and spinach au gratin, for around 90–140dh a throw.

# Accommodation

For many people, the main reason for coming to Marrakesh is to stay in a riad. These are stylish Medina guesthouses, mostly quite upmarket, and often very exclusive – for more on them, see the box opposite. The Medina is also the place to find top-notch palatial hotels, such as *La Mamounia* and the *Maison Arabe*, as well as the widest range of characterful mid-range hotels, usually in refurbished houses with en-suite rooms priced at 350–650dh. Most budget hotels are near the Jemaa el Fna, with double rooms for as little as 150–200dh a night, usually with shared bathrooms. Modern three-, four- and five-star hotels are concentrated in Guéliz and Hivernage; standards of service in the Hivernage package hotels are frankly amateurish, though they do offer wheelchair access, big pools and a child-friendly atmosphere. For more tranquil surroundings than you'll find in the city centre, it's worth considering hotels in Semlalia, at the northern end of the Ville Nouvelle, or better still, a place out in the Palmery to the northeast. Essaouira has a similar range of accommodation, including some lovely low-key riads, rather cheaper than those in Marrakesh, while sleeping options up in the Atlas mountains tend to be rougher and readier, mostly cheap little hotels and mountain refuges, though you can also stay in a former local chieftain's palace.

## The Jemaa el Fna and the Koutoubia

**HOTEL ADAY** > 111 Derb Sidi Bouloukat ☎ 0524 441920, ⓦ hotel-aday.com. MAP P.36–37, POCKET MAP B12. This friendly budget hotel is well kept, clean and pleasantly decorated. Rooms with shared facilities are grouped around a central patio, and are small, with most having only inward-facing windows, but there's hot water round the clock, and also a newer wing with more comfortable, en-suite rooms. Alternatively, in summer, you can sleep on the roof for 35dh. Rates exclude breakfast. 154dh.

**HOTEL ALI** > Rue Moulay Ismail ☎ 0524 444979, ⓦ hotel-ali.com. MAP P.36–37, POCKET MAP B12. This busy hotel is used by groups heading to the High Atlas, so it's a good source of trekking (and other) information, and staff are always extremely helpful. They also change money, and can arrange car, minibus or 4WD rental, and there is free wi-fi. The place has a general air of business and being right in the middle of things, though that won't appeal to everyone. Rooms are en suite with a/c but very simple decor; they also vary in size, and some of them can get a bit whiffy in summer, so it's wise to check before taking one. Booking ahead is advisable. From 360dh.

# Riads

There are now hundreds of riads in Marrakesh, though they vary in quality, so it's worth shopping around. Literally, a "riad" means a patio garden, but the term has become synonymous with an upmarket guesthouse in a refurbished old mansion, whether it has a patio garden or not.

The trend started in the 1990s, when Europeans who'd bought houses in the Medina for their own use discovered they could make a pretty penny by taking in paying guests. Since then, the whole thing has escalated into something of an industry (a bubble waiting to burst in the eyes of some), and it's spread to other Moroccan cities, most notably Fez and Essaouira.

Riads range from plain and simple lodgings in a Moroccan family home (often called **maisons d'hôtes**, French for "guest house") to restored old mansions with classic decor. Many European-owned riads have been made up to look like something from an interior-design magazine, with swimming pools in the patio and jacuzzis on the roof. The best riads are stamped with the personality of the people who own them, often a couple or family who live alongside, and can be a good way to get a feel for Moroccan life.

## Riad booking agencies

**Marrakesh Medina** 102 Rue Dar el Bacha, Northern Medina ☎ 0524 290707, ⓦ marrakech-medina.com. A firm that's actually in the business of doing up riads as well as renting them out, with a reasonable selection in all price ranges.

**Marrakech Riads** *Dar Cherifa*, 8 Derb Charfa Lakbir, Mouassine, Northern Medina ☎ 0524 426463, ⓦ marrakech-riads.net. A small agency with only eight riads; committed to keeping it chic and authentic.

**Riads au Maroc** 13 Derb el Ferrane, Riad el Arous, Northern Medina ☎ 0524 378156, ⓦ riadsaumaroc.com. One of the first and biggest riad agencies with lots of choice in all price categories.

**HOTEL CENTRAL PALACE** ➤ 59 Derb Sidi Bouloukat ☎ 0524 440235, ⓦ lecentralpalace.com MAP P.36–37, POCKET MAP B12. The rooms here are a cut above those in the other budget hotels in the back alleys south of the Jemaa el Fna, and correspondingly slightly pricier, but what this place also has going for it (aside from an in-house pizzeria and travel agency) is its easy-to-find location, just off Rue Bab Agnaou, a stone's throw from the Jemaa. Rates exclusive of breakfast. From 155dh.

**HOTEL CTM** ➤ Jemaa el Fna ☎ 0524 442325. MAP P.36–37, POCKET MAP B12.

*Hotel CTM* is above the old bus station (hence its name), which is now used as a car park, so it's handy if you're driving. There are currently three categories of rooms: old and unmodernized with shared bathroom or en suite, clean but drab, with hot-water showers (200dh); and modernized and en suite with a/c in summer, heating in winter (300dh). The last category includes rooms 1–4, which overlook the square, giving you your own private view, though this does of course make them noisy. Breakfast is served on the roof terrace, which also looks over the square. From 200dh.

## Accommodation prices

Seasons vary slightly from establishment to establishment, but in general, **high season** for Marrakesh accommodation means March–May plus September and October; note that rates over the **Christmas/New Year** period can be as much as fifty percent higher than in the rest of the high season. The rates quoted here – which include **breakfast** unless otherwise stated – are for the cheapest double room in high season (excluding Christmas and New Year); the rest of the year, you can expect prices to be anything from ten to fifty percent cheaper. Most hotels fix their prices in dirhams, but some upmarket establishments fix them in euros or even pounds. For these places we've included the dirham price in brackets, and note that in all cases you'll be able to pay in local currency.

**HOTEL DE FOUCAULD** > Av el Mouahidine ☎ 0524 440806, ✉ hoteldefoucauld@gmail.com. MAP P.36–37, POCKET MAP A13. Rooms are a little sombre and some are a bit on the small side, but they're decent enough, with a/c, heating and constant hot water (with a choice of tub or shower). There's a roof terrace with views of the Koutoubia, and a restaurant with buffet suppers. The staff can arrange tours, help with local information and put you onto guides for High Atlas trekking. Excludes breakfast. 295dh.

**HOTEL ESSAOUIRA** > 3 Derb Sidi Bouloukat ☎ 0524 443805. MAP P.36–37, POCKET MAP B12. This is one of the most popular cheapies in Marrakesh – and with good reason. It's a well-run, safe place, with thirty rooms, communal hot showers, a laundry service, baggage deposit and rooftop café. Rates exclude breakfast. 100dh.

**HOTEL GALLIA** > 30 Rue de la Recette ☎ 0524 445913, ⓦ hotelgallia.com. MAP P.36–37, POCKET MAP B13. A beautifully kept hotel in a restored Medina mansion, the *Gallia* has immaculate en-suite rooms off two tiled courtyards, one with a fountain, palm tree and caged birds. There's central heating in winter and a/c in summer. It's a long-time favourite and highly recommended. Book online, at least a month ahead if possible. Rates exclude breakfast. 460dh.

**HOTEL ICHBILIA** > 1 Rue Ben Marine ☎ 0524 381530 MAP P.36–37, POCKET MAP B12. Near the Cinéma Mabrouka, and well placed for shops, banks and cafés, the *Ichbilia* has rooms off a covered gallery. Some are plain and simple, but still clean and comfortable, others have a/c and private bathroom. Some locals will know it as the *Hotel Sevilla*, Ichbilia being the Arabic for Seville. Rates exclude breakfast. 180–320dh.

**HOTEL LA MAMOUNIA** > Av Bab Jedid ☎ 0524 388600, ⓦ mamounia .com MAP P.36–37, POCKET MAP E6. Set in palatial grounds, this is Marrakesh's most famous hotel, and its most expensive, with an emphasis on opulence and exclusivity. Decoratively, it is of most interest for the 1920s Art Deco touches by Jacques Majorelle (of Majorelle Garden fame), and their enhancements, in 1986, by the then Moroccan king's favourite designer, André Paccard. The rooms are done out in warm reds and browns, with magnificent marble bathrooms, but some of the simple "classic" rooms can be on the small side, so it's best to pay a bit more for a "superior" or "deluxe" (and there's a range of suites and riads costing up to ten times more). *La Maison Arabe* (see p.108) is generally better value if you're looking to be pampered, but it can't match the *Mamounia*'s facilities or architectural splendour. Doubles start at 5599dh excluding breakfast.

**HOTEL MEDINA** > 1 Derb Sidi Bouloukat ☎ 0524 442997, ⓦ hotelmedinamarrakech.com. MAP

P.36–37, POCKET MAP B12. Located in a street full of good budget hotels, the *Medina* is a perennial favourite among the cheapies, and often full. It's clean, friendly and pretty good value, and there's always hot water in the shared showers. The owner – who used to work in Britain as a circus acrobat – speaks good English. They have a small roof terrace and in summer there's also the option of sleeping on the roof (30dh). 110dh.

**HOTEL SHERAZADE** > 3 Derb Djama, off Rue Riad Zitoun el Kadim ☎ 0524 429305, W hotelsherazade.com. MAP P.36–37, POCKET MAP B12. This old merchant's house, attractively done up, was already on the scene before riads took off big time. Besides a lovely roof terrace, the hotel offers a wide variety of well-maintained rooms in pretty pastel colours, not all en suite. Run very professionally by a German-Moroccan couple, it's extremely popular, so book well ahead. Rates exclude breakfast. From 330dh.

**JNANE MOGADOR HOTEL** > Derb Sidi Bouloukat, by 116 Rue Riad Zitoun el Kadim ☎ 0524 426323, W jnanemogador.com. MAP P.36–37, POCKET MAP B12. Run by the same management as the *Essaouira*, this more upmarket hostelry is just as homely and is already establishing itself as a favourite among Marrakesh's mid-range accommodation. Set in a beautifully restored old house, it boasts charming rooms, in warm tints with modern furnishings, around a lovely fountain patio, its own hammam and a roof terrace where you can have breakfast, or tea and cake. 480dh.

**RIAD ZINOUN** > 31 Derb Ben Amrane, off Rue Riad Zitoun el Kadim ☎ 0524 426793, W riadzinoun.com. MAP P.36–37, POCKET MAP C13. A friendly little riad, run by a French-Moroccan couple, the *Zinoun* isn't the most chic of its kind in the Medina, but this nicely refurbished old house is agreeably relaxing, with a pleasant central patio (covered in winter, open in summer), and rooms decorated with rugs and traditional painted-wood furniture. From €64.50 (700dh).

# The Northern Medina

**DAR EL ASSAFIR** > 24bis Arset el Hamed ☎ 0524 387377, W riaddarelassafir.com. MAP P.46–47, POCKET MAP E4. Located behind the town hall, in a part of the Medina open to traffic, this is a late nineteenth-century colonial mansion decorated in colonial rather than traditional style. It's quite spacious, with two patios and a nice pool, singing birds in a little aviary and *belle époque*-style rooms with orientalist ornaments. From €75 (800dh).

**DAR IHSSANE** > 14 Derb Chorfa el Kebir, near Mouassine Mosque ☎ 0524 387826, W dar-ihssane.com. MAP P.46–47, POCKET MAP B11. *Dar Ihssane* is a good-value riad in an eighteenth-century mansion with many original features (some of which were only discovered during renovation), and small but light and airy rooms. It's owned by the nephew of painter Georges Bretegnier, and is decorated with some of Bretegnier's original paintings and drawings. From 330dh.

**DAR MOUASSINE** > 148 Derb Essnane, off Rue Sidi el Yamami ☎ 0524 445287, W darmouassine .com. MAP P.46–47, POCKET MAP A11. The rooms here have classic Moroccan decor, the salon and the patio (which also has a fountain and banana trees) less so. There are well-chosen and interesting prints on the walls, all rooms have CD players, and the better ones have painted wooden ceilings. From €105 (1140dh).

**DAR SALAM** > 162 Derb Ben Fayda, off Rue el Gza near Bab Doukkala ☎ 0524 384141, E rayadsalam@yahoo .fr. MAP P.46–47, POCKET MAP F3. This is a true *maison d'hôte* as opposed to a riad: a Moroccan family home that takes in guests, and a place to relax and put your feet up rather than admire the decor. The food is similarly unpretentious – tasty home-style Moroccan cooking, like your mum would make if she were Marrakshi. From €30 (326dh).

**DAR SILSILA** > 11 Derb Jedid el Kabir, off Rue Sidi el Yamani ☎ 0645 900781, ⓦ darsilsila.com. MAP P.46-47, POCKET MAP A11. Though a smallish Medina house, *Dar Silsila* has lots of corners in which to hide away. It's Moroccan in style with good use of Iraqi-style coloured glass plus European and West African touches, and two of the nine rooms have a sub-Saharan theme, celebrating the French owner's previous sojourn in Guinea and the Congo. From €146 (1559dh).

**EQUITY POINT MARRAKECH** > 80 Derb el Hammam Mouassine ☎ 0524 440793, ⓦ equity-point.com. MAP P.46-47. POCKET MAP B11. A hostel in a riad, with all the architectural charm of any other riad, but a fun crowd and four- to eight-bed dorms instead of the usual flowers-on-the-pillow service. There's wi-fi, a pool, a bar and a restaurant, cool spaces to hang out in, and a friendly atmosphere. Dorms €13 (141dh), doubles €65 (705dh).

**LA MAISON ARABE** > 1 Derb Assehbi Bab Doukkala, behind the Doukkala Mosque ☎ 0524 387010, ⓦ lamaisonarabe.com. MAP P.46-47, POCKET MAP E4. Though not as famous as the *Mamounia*, this is arguably Marrakesh's classiest hotel, a gorgeous nineteenth-century mansion that's been restored with fine traditional workmanship. The furnishings are classic Moroccan and sumptuous, as is the food (it even offers cookery classes), and standards of service are high. There are two beautifully kept patios and a selection of rooms and suites, all in warm colours with comfortable modern furnishings, some with private terrace and jacuzzi. There is no pool on the premises, but a free shuttle bus can take you to the hotel's private pool nearby. Rates include afternoon tea as well as breakfast. From 2500dh.

**NOIR D'IVOIRE** > 31 Derb Jedid, Bab Doukkala ☎ 0524 380975, ⓦ noir-d-ivoire.com. MAP P.46-47, POCKET MAP F4. This magnificent riad is impressive from the moment you walk in. It's owned by an English interior designer, who's decorated it in cream, brown and black (the name refers to the colour scheme), with a feel that manages to be both classic and modern, classy yet cosy, all at the same time. There's a well-equipped gym, two pools and a bar, and service is punctilious, reflecting the fact that there's almost one staff member per guest. From 2257dh.

**RIAD 72** > 72 Derb Arset Aouzal ☎ 0524 387629, ⓦ riad72.com. MAP P.46-47, POCKET MAP F4. This Italian-owned riad is sleek and stylish, with sparse but very tasteful modern decor, palms and banana trees in the courtyard and its own hammam (but no pool). The catering is Moroccan. It's part of a group called Uovo (Italian for "egg") who have a similarly stylish sister establishment, *Riad Due* at 2 Derb Chentouf (ⓦ riaddue.com). Rates include breakfast, afternoon tea and one airport transfer. From €160 (1775dh).

**RIAD AL MASSARAH** > 26 Derb Jedid, Bab Doukkala ☎ 0524 383206, ⓦ riadalmassarah.com. MAP P.46-47, POCKET MAP E4. Light defines this cool, airy riad. It's done out in white, and rather minimalist, but for all that it's small, friendly and quite intimate, and the owners (one French, one British) are great hosts. There's solar-heated water, a pool and a real fire in most rooms. The riad encourages responsible tourism and supports local charities. Rates include breakfast and afternoon tea. From 1246dh.

**RIAD ELIZABETH** > 33 Derb el Baroud, Hart Essoura ☎ 0641 229935, ⓦ riadelizabeth.com. MAP P.46-47, POCKET MAP H4. Elegant but homely, this good-value and very friendly riad is run by an English couple (she designed it, he built it), with a strong personal touch, lots of cool black-and-white decor, disco-style mirror-mosaic loos, a large patio pool and a spacious roof terrace. Each room is different, but all are modern and bright. Parking nearby. From €130 (1385dh).

**RIAD EL MANSOUR** > 227 Derb Jedid, Bab Doukkala ☎ 0524 381577, ⓦ riadelmansour.com. MAP P.46-47,

POCKET MAP E3. This British-owned riad prides itself on service rather than decor, though it's got plenty of carved cedar and wooden ceilings, as well as a shaded patio, jaccuzzi and gym, hammam and massage room. You get fresh and dried fruits and Moroccan pastries in your room every day, and the staff are extremely attentive. Rates include free airport transfer as well as breakfast. From €130 (1388dh).

### RIAD FARNATCHI > 2 Derb el
Farnatchi, off Rue Bin Lafnadek ☎ 0524 384910, Ⓦ riadfarnatchi .com. MAP P.46–47, POCKET MAP C10. The suites (there are no ordinary rooms) at this efficient and professionally run British-owned riad are spacious, each with either a balcony, a private terrace or its own patio, though the understated decor incorporates some quite rustic features. There are also two common patios, one with a pool, and the salons and dining rooms are very stylish. Rates include breakfast, free airport transfer, free hot and cold drinks, and canapés before dinner. From 3400dh.

### RIAD KHEIRREDINE > 2 Derb
Chelligui, Sidi Ben Slimane ☎ 0524 386364, Ⓦ riadkheirredine.com. MAP P.46–47, POCKET MAP F3. Super-cool and very welcoming Italian-run riad (although most of the guests are from English-speaking countries), with two patios and two pools, rooms and public spaces done out in delicious creams and dark chocolate browns, in a residential part of the Medina, very handy for the Majorelle Garden and the bus station .The staff go out of their way to be as helpful as possible. From €150 (1627dh).

### RIAD KNIZA > 34 Derb l'Hotel,
near Bab Doukkala ☎ 0524 376942, riadkniza.com. MAP P.46–47, POCKET MAP E4. Owned by a top antique dealer and tour guide (whose clients have included US presidents and film stars), this is one classy riad. The rooms are beautiful, with classic Moroccan decor, and there's a state-of-the-art pool, not to mention a sauna, hammam and massage room, real antiques for decoration, and

solar panels for ecologically sound hot water – yet it still manages to feel like a real Moroccan family home. The family themselves (all English-speaking) are always on hand to make you feel welcome, the food is excellent and the service is absolutely impeccable. Rates include breakfast and airport transfers. From €225 (2395dh).

### RIAD LES TROIS PALMIERS >
36 Derb Tizougarine, near Dar el Bacha ☎ 0600 024560, Ⓦ riadlestroispalmiers.com. MAP P.46–47, POCKET MAP A10. Two adjoining eighteenth-century mansions, originally built for two branches of the same family, have now been reunited to make this graceful riad. The decor is predominantly brown and cream, with lots of original features including a lovely painted ceiling, and the three palms that give the riad its name, which grow in one of the two patios. Under French ownership though English is spoken too. Prices include breakfast. From €69 (737dh).

### RIAD MALIKA > 29–36 Derb Arset
Aouzal ☎ 0524 385451, Ⓦ riadmalika .com. MAP P.46–47, POCKET MAP F4. Sumptuous decor – modern but with colonial and 1930s touches – bedecks this very stylish riad owned by architect and interior designer Jean-Luc Lemée. There's loads of chequered tiling, a lovely pool, a warm salon and plush bedroom furnishings. It's very popular and needs booking well ahead. From €110 (1175dh).

### RIAD PAPILLON > 15 Derb
Tizougarine, near Dar el Bacha ☎ 0614 234965, reservations UK ☎ +44 20 7193 7357, US ☎ +1 800 845 0810, Ⓦ riadpapillon.com. MAP P.46–47, POCKET MAP B10. The staff go out of their way to help you feel at home in this small but very friendly riad. They also keep the place scented with jasmine oil, which you may or may not like. The rooms are named after flowers, but rather than being frilly are sparsely yet tastefully decorated with small touches. The same firm also run the Henna Café (see p.56) and Riad Star (see p.110). From €100 (1284dh).

**RIAD SAFA** > 64 Derb Lalla Azouna, off Rue Essebtiyne ☏ 0524 377123, ⓦ riad-safa.com. MAP P.46–47, POCKET MAP H4. There's a sun-bleached look to this small, rather unassuming, rustic-feeling riad, with lots of whitewash and unvarnished wood, plus a few sparse splashes of colour. It's also quite intimate, with only five rooms and two patios. There's also a roof terrace complete with jacuzzi and of course an in-house hammam, but what really makes this a great place to stay is the personal attention of the two (English-speaking) French owners. From €80 (861dh).

**RIAD SAHARA NOUR** > 118 Derb Dekkak ☏ 0524 376570, ⓦ riadsaharanour-marrakech.com. MAP P.46–47, POCKET MAP E4. More than just a riad, this is a centre for art, self-development and relaxation. Art workshops in music, dance, painting and calligraphy are held here, and self-development programmes in meditation and relaxation techniques are available. Guests who wish to hold artistic happenings are encouraged, but you don't need to take part in these activities in order to stay here and enjoy the calm atmosphere on the patio, shaded by orange, loquat and pomegranate trees. From €79.60 (847dh).

**RIAD STAR** 31 Derb Alailich (off Rue de Souk des Fassis) ☏ 0656 566374, UK T020 7193 7357, USA T1 800 845 0810, ⓦ riadstar.com. MAP P.46–47, POCKET MAP C10. Run by the same people as Riad Papillon (see p.109) and the Henna Café (see p.56), this is the former home of jazz dancer Josephine Baker, who lived here during World War Two, when she was a spy for Free France, the riad is themed on her era, with memorabilia and even costumes that you can wear. The rooms are stylish, with black tiled bathrooms and there's an in-house hammam and a rooftop sun terrace. From £140 (2113dh).

**RIAD ZOLAH** > 114–116 Derb el Hammam, near Mouassine Mosque ☏ 0524 387535, ⓦ riadzolah.com. MAP P.46–47, POCKET MAP B11. An English-owned riad run with flair by a vivacious English-speaking Moroccan

## Hammams

Even the cheapest hotels in Marrakesh have bathroom facilities, sometimes shared, but for a really Moroccan bathing experience, it's worth trying a hammam.

A hammam is a Turkish-style **steam bath**, with a succession of rooms ranging in temperature from cool to hot, and endless supplies of hot and cold water, which you fetch in buckets. The usual procedure is to find a piece of floor space in the hot room, surround it with as many buckets of water as you feel you need, and lie in the heat to sweat out the dirt from your pores before scrubbing it off. A plastic bowl is useful for scooping the water from the buckets to wash with. You can also order a **massage**, in which you will be allowed to sweat, pulled about a bit to relax your muscles, and then rigorously scrubbed with a rough flannel glove (*kiis*). Alternatively, buy a *kiis* and do it yourself. Note that complete **nudity** is taboo, so you should keep your underwear on (bring a dry change) or wear a swimming costume, and change with a towel around you.

For many Moroccan **women**, who would not go out to a café or bar, the hammam is a social gathering place, in which women tourists are made very welcome too. Indeed, hammams turn out to be a highlight for many women travellers, and an excellent way to make contact with Moroccan women.

manager, this is really a lovely place to stay. You get a free pair of Moroccan slippers when you arrive, fresh and dried fruit in your room daily and all sorts of little touches that make you feel like a special guest ("the most generous range of extras in Marrakesh", so they claim). Facilities include wi-fi, in-house hammam and massage room, and the decor is tasteful with lots of white, generous splashes of colour, original features and wonderful use of carpets and drapes. Rates include breakfast and airport transfers. From 2257dh.

**RIYAD EL CADI** > 86–87 Derb Moulay Abdelkader, off Rue Dabachi ☎ 0524 378098, ⓦ riyadelcadi.com. MAP P.46–47, POCKET MAP C11. The former home of a German diplomat who was ambassador to several Arab countries, the *El Cadi* is embellished with his wonderful collection of rugs and antiques. It incorporates five patios, three salons, a pool, a hammam, and there's free wi-fi and excellent standards of service. The rooms vary in style, each having a theme (camels in the Camel Room, for example) on which the decor is based, and as well as ordinary guest rooms, there are two wonderful suites, and the "blue house", a patio with two double rooms, which is rented in its entirety. From €140 (1490dh).

## The Southern Medina and Agdal Gardens

**DAR LES CIGOGNES** > 108 Rue Berrima ☎ 0524 382740, ⓦ lescigognes.com. MAP P.62–63, POCKET MAP H7. This luxury boutique hotel, run by a Swiss–American couple, gets consistently good reports. It takes the form of two converted Medina houses done up in traditional fashion around the patio, but with modern decor in the rooms and suites. Features include a library, a hammam, a jacuzzi, a salon and a terrace where you can see storks nesting on the walls of the royal palace opposite (hence the name, which means "house of the storks"), and cookery lessons are available. All rooms are en suite; from €227 (2411dh).

There are quite a lot of hammams in the Medina; the three closest to the Jemaa el Fna (all south of the square) are **Hammam Polo** on Rue de la Recette; **Hammam Sidi Bouloukate**, just round the corner from *Hotel Central Palace*; and one (unsigned) at the northern end of Rue Riad Zitoun el Kadim. All three are open from 6am to 8pm for women and the same or slightly longer for men, with separate entrances for each sex, and all cost 12dh. Don't forget to bring along some soap and shampoo (though these are often sold at the hammam), and a towel (these are sometimes rented, but can be a bit dubious).

In addition to ordinary Moroccan hammams, there are also upmarket tourist hammams such as **Hammam Ziani**, 14 Rue Riad Zitoun el Jedid (☎ 0662 715571, ⓦ hammamziani.ma; daily 7am–10pm), open for both sexes (separate areas), costing 50dh for a simple steam bath, or 350dh for an all-in package with massage. Even posher is **Les Bains de Marrakech**, 2 Derb Sedra, down an alley by Bab Agnaou in the Kasbah (☎ 0524 381428, ⓦ lesbainsdemarrakech.com; daily 9am–7.30pm), where prices start at 200dh and you'll need to book in advance. Despite these high prices, you won't (unless you're gay) be able to share a steam bath experience with your partner – if you want to do that, you'll have to stay at one of the many riads listed in this chapter with their own in-house hammam.

**LA SULTANA** > 403 Rue de la Kasbah 🕿 0524 388008, 🌐 lasultanamarrakech .com. MAP P.62–63, POCKET MAP G7. For those who can't decide between a riad, a five-star or a boutique hotel, this is an extremely stylish blend of all three: riad style, boutique personal attention and five-star facilities. Facilities include a hammam, pool, jacuzzi, spa, lounge bar, library, panoramic terraces and excellent dining – all just round the corner from Bab Agnaou and the Saadian Tombs. Rates exclude breakfast. From 4400dh.

**LE CLOS DES ARTS** > 50 Derb Tbib, off Rue Riad Zitoun el Jedid 🕿 0524 375159, 🌐 leclosdesarts.com. MAP P.62–63, POCKET MAP C13. This beautiful riad is filled with the works of one of the proprietors, who is a painter and sculptor as well as an interior designer. Each room has its own style and colour, and the whole effect is warm and delightful, as are the owners, who give it a real personal touch. Workshops on Moroccan art techniques are available €120.50 (1297dh).

**LES JARDINS DE LA MEDINA** > 21 Derb Chtouka, Kasbah 🕿 0524 381851, 🌐 lesjardinsdelamedina .com. MAP P.62–63, POCKET MAP G9. This beautiful old palace has been transformed into a truly sumptuous hotel. The 36 rooms, each with its own character and individual decor, are set around an extensive patio garden with hammocks slung between the trees and a decent-sized pool. What the hotel really plugs, however, is its hammam-cum-beauty salon where you can get manicured, pedicured, scrubbed and massaged till you glow. From 2357dh.

**RIAD AGUERZAME** > 66 Derb Jedid, Douar Graoua 🕿 0524 381184. 🌐 riadaguerzame.com. MAP P.62–63, POCKET MAP H6. A small, intimate riad – only four rooms – with a personal touch supplied by its genial, English-speaking Breton host, who's invariably on hand to look after you, and dispense local advice and information about the neighbourhood. It's one of a trio of small riads (see 🌐 bestriadmarrakech.com) run by three friends with similar ideas, so if it's full, you could try the others (Riad Limouna

and Riad Menzeh). Doubles start at €82 (912dh), and readers of this book are promised any room for the same rate.

**RIAD & SPA BAHIA SALAM** > 61 Av Houmane el Fetouaki 🕿 0524 426060, 🌐 riadbahiasalam.com. MAP P.62–63, POCKET MAP G7. Despite its name, this converted nineteenth-century mansion, decorated in Marrakesh red ochre with lots of zellij and carved cedar, is really a good-value and quite stylish hotel rather than a riad. Its main attraction is its full range of hammam and spa facilities, though the rooms are modern and elegant. It's also very centrally located, with parking directly across the street. From 1052dh.

**RIAD AKKA** > 65 Derb Lahbib Magni, off Rue de la Bahia 🕿 0524 375767, 🌐 riad-akka-marrakech.com. MAP P.62–63, POCKET MAP H6. Orange, grey and black decor characterize the public areas of this stylish, modern riad, where all of the furniture was designed by one of the French owners and there's a different colour scheme for every room. It's particularly favoured by golfing enthusiasts, but pleasing to anyone with a sense of style. From €120 (1292dh).

**RIAD BAYTI** > 35 Derb Saka, Bab el Mellah 🕿 0524 380180, 🌐 riad-bayti .com. MAP P.62–63, POCKET MAP H7. The high ceilings and wide veranda typical of old Mellah houses give a spacious feel to this riad, formerly owned by a family of Jewish wine merchants. Run by a dynamic young French couple, its warm modern decor perfectly complements the classic architecture and the smell of spices wafting in from the market below. Facilities include free childcare and wi-fi. Rates include breakfast and afternoon tea. From €94 (1000dh).

**RIAD DAR ONE** > 19 Derb Jemaa el Kebir, Mellah 🕿 0600 021381, 🌐 riad-dar-one.com. MAP P.62–63, POCKET MAP H7. This old Mellah house has been renovated in quite minimalist modern style, with beige, brown and white decor, and lashings of tadelakt (see p.135). It's very handy for sights like the Bahia and El Badi palaces, and the owner is usually on hand to make you feel at home and give help and advice. From €130 (1400dh).

**RIYAD AL MOUSSIKA** > 62 Derb Boutouil, Kennaria ☎ 0524 389067, Ⓦ riyad-al-moussika.ma. MAP P.62–63, POCKET MAP C12. This gem of a riad was formerly owned by French former governor, Thami el Glaoui. A harmonious and beautiful combination of Moroccan tradition and Italian flair, its decor is gorgeous – like a traditional Marrakshi mansion, but better. The walls are decked with local art, and the Italian owner's son, a cordon bleu chef, takes care of the catering – in fact, the riad claims to have the finest cuisine in town. Rate includes breakfast, lunch and afternoon tea. 2500dh.

**VILLA DES ORANGERS** > 6 Rue Sidi Mimoun, off Pl Youssef Ben Tachfine ☎ 0524 384638, Ⓦ villadesorangers .com. MAP P.62–63, POCKET MAP F7. Officially classified as a hotel, this place is in fact a riad in the true sense of the term: an old house around a patio garden (three gardens in fact), with orange trees and a complete overdose of lovely carved stucco. There's a range of rooms and suites – many with their own private terrace – as well as three pools (one on the roof), two restaurants and a spacious salon with a real fireplace. A light lunch, as well as breakfast, is included in the price. From €418 (4441dh).

# The Ville Nouvelle and Palmery

**DAR ZEMORA** > 72 Rue el Aandalib, Palmery, 3km from town ☎ 0524 328200, reservations UK ☎ +44 20 7583 9265, Ⓦ darzemora.com. MAP P.73, POCKET MAP J1. This British-owned luxury villa, stylishly embellished with a mix of traditional and modern features, has a pleasant garden with a pool, a masseur on call and a view of the Atlas mountains from the roof terrace. All rooms have CD players though no TV. To find it, take the next left (Rue Qortoba) off the Route de Fès after the Circuit de la Palmeraie, then the first right (Rue el Yassamin), fork left after 300m and it's 300m round the bend on the right. Breakfast and afternoon tea included. £195 (2853dh).

**HOTEL AKABAR** > Av Echouhada, Hivernage ☎ 0524 437799, Ⓦ hotel akabar.ma. MAP P.73, POCKET MAP D5. A friendly little three-star with a smallish pool and reasonably priced restaurant, handy for both the Medina and the Ville Nouvelle. The rooms (with a/c and satellite TV) are small but cool, and it's worth taking one at the back if you don't like noise. 500dh, excluding breakfast.

**HOTEL ATLAS MEDINA** > Av Moulay el Hassan, Hivernage ☎ 0524 339999, Ⓦ www.hotelsatlas.com. MAP P.73, POCKET MAP B6. Set amid extensive gardens planted with no fewer than two hundred palm trees, this is the Atlas chain's top offering in Marrakesh. It's best known for its spa facilities, which offer treatments using traditional Moroccan hammam cosmetics such as *ghassoul* mud-shampoo, here used for a facial rather than to wash hair. Rooms are modern and carpeted, with cosy red and orange decor. From 1150dh.

**HOTEL DES VOYAGEURS** > 40 Bd Mohammed Zerktouni, Guéliz ☎ 0524 447218. MAP P.73, POCKET MAP A14. This old budget hotel with an Art Deco façade feels like it's caught in a time warp, but it's well kept, with spacious if rather sombre rooms and a pleasant little garden. Quiet and peaceful despite being located right in the heart of Guéliz. Breakfast excluded. From 144dh.

**HOTEL DU PACHA** > 33 Rue de la Liberté, Guéliz ☎ 0524 431327, Ⓦ hotelpacha.net. MAP P.73, POCKET MAP B14. Built in the 1930s, the *Du Pacha* has large if rather drab rooms, most around a central courtyard, with a/c and satellite TV. There's a good restaurant, but no pool. 417.60dh.

**HOTEL FAROUK** > 66 Av Hassan II, Guéliz ☎ 0524 431989, Ⓦ hotelfarouk .com. MAP P.73, POCKET MAP B15. Housed in a rather eccentric building, with all sorts of extensions, the *Farouk* offers a variety of rooms – have a look at a few before choosing – all with hot showers. Staff are friendly and there's an excellent restaurant. Owned by the same family as the *Ali* in the Medina. Prices exclusive of breakfast. 210dh.

**HOTEL FASHION** > 45 Av Hassan II, Guéliz ☎ 0524 423707, 🖂 fashionhotel @hotmail.fr. MAP P.73, POCKET MAP B15. Terracotta tiling, nicely carved black-painted wooden furnishings and large windows grace the rooms at this tastefully designed three-star, where the bathrooms feature reliable hot showers with a strong jet. There's also a rooftop pool and basement hammam. 550dh.

**HOTEL PALMERAIE GOLF PALACE** > Circuit de la Palmeraie, off Route de Casablanca, 5km from town ☎ 0524 334343, 🌐 pgpmarrakech.com. MAP P.73, POCKET MAP D1. The *Palmeraie Golf Palace* has five (small) swimming pools, plus squash and tennis courts, a bowling alley, riding stables, and most importantly, its own eighteen-hole golf course. Officially a five-star, it was a favourite with Morocco's late king, Hassan II, though most tourists find it rather corporate and impersonal. The rooms are elegant and split-level, with beds raised above the sitting area. From 1650dh.

**HOTEL TICHKA** > Off Bd Mohammed Abdelkrim el Khattabi, Semlalia, about 1km north of the junction with Av Mohammed V (served by bus #1 from the Koutoubia) ☎ 0524 448710, 🌐 hotel-marrakech-tichka.com. MAP P.73, POCKET MAP A1. Built in 1986, this hotel boasts decor by Tunisian architect Charles Boccara and American interior designer Bill Willis, including columns in the form of stylized palm trees reminiscent of ancient Egypt. Most notable is the use of tadelakt (see p.135), the employment of which here by Willis made it massively trendy in Moroccan interior design (most riads use lots of it). Rooms are modern and cosy, in brown and cream, and the hotel has a swimming pool, a health centre and its own hammam, and one room is adapted for wheelchair users. The staff are friendly but the hotel is getting a bit worn around the edges. 2167.26dh, excluding breakfast. Big discounts often available online.

**HOTEL TOULOUSAIN** > 44 Rue Tarik Ben Ziad, Guéliz ☎ 0524 430033, 🌐 hoteltoulousain.com. MAP P.73, POCKET MAP B14. This excellent budget hotel was originally owned by a Frenchman from Toulouse (hence the name). It has a secure car park, free wi-fi and a variety of rooms, plainly decorated but always spick and span. Some have shower, some shower and toilet and some shared facilities; some have ceiling fans too. From 220dh.

**IBIS MARRAKECH CENTRE GARE** > Av Hassan II/Pl de la Gare, Guéliz ☎ 0524 435929, 🌐 ibishotel.com. MAP P.73, POCKET MAP A4. This tasteful chain hotel located right by the train station is not the most exciting accommodation in town, but it's good value. It offers efficient service, a swimming pool, a restaurant and a bar in the lobby, and good buffet breakfasts are available. 800dh.

**LES DEUX TOURS** > Douar Abiad, Circuit de la Palmeraie, 4km from town ☎ 0524 329525, 🌐 les-deux-tours .com. MAP P.73, POCKET MAP J1. The *deux tours* (two towers) of the name flank the gateway to this cluster of luxury *villas d'hôte* designed by locally renowned architect Charles Boccara. Located in an open patch of the Palmery, and not signposted (take a turn-off to the east about halfway along the Route de la Palmeraie, signposted "Villa des Trois Golfs", then continue for about 600m, ignoring any further signs to the *Trois Golfs*), this is a beautiful, tranquil spot, with four rooms to each villa, all built in traditional Moroccan brick and decorated in restful earth colours, each villa with its own little garden. There's a hammam, swimming pool, restaurant and bar, as well as extensive shared gardens in which to wander or relax. From €191 (2057dh).

**THE RED HOUSE** > Bd el Yarmouk, opposite the city wall, Hivernage ☎ 0524 437040, 🌐 theredhousemarrakech.com. MAP P.73, POCKET MAP E6. This beautiful nineteenth-century mansion (also called *Dar el Ahmar*) is awash with fine stucco and zellij work downstairs, where the restaurant offers gourmet Moroccan cuisine (see p.84). Accommodation consists of eight luxurious suites – extremely chic and palatial – though imperial European rather than classic Moroccan in style. From 1900dh.

**RYAD MOGADOR MENARA** > Av Mohammed VI (Av de France), Hivernage ☎ 0524 339330, Ⓦ www .ryadmogador.com. MAP P.73, POCKET MAP B6. The facilities at this five-star hotel (though it's really more like a four-star) include a health club and three restaurants. The lobby is decorated in classic style, with painted ceilings, chandeliers and a very Moroccan feel, and the receptionists wear traditional garb. Rooms, on the other hand, are modern, light and airy. There's also a babysitting service. 2035dh.

**SOFITEL MARRAKECH** > Rue Harroun Errachid, Hivernage ☎ 0524 425600, Ⓦ www.sofitel.com. MAP P.73, POCKET MAP D6. This chain hotel is not up to Western five-star standards, but it isn't too bad as package hotels go. It's done out in royal red, with two restaurants, two bars, three pools and a fitness centre with a sauna, jacuzzi and hammam. Rates exclude breakfast. €380.

**YOUTH HOSTEL (AUBERGE DE JEUNESSE)** > Rue el Jahed, Hivernage ☎ 0524 447713, Ⓦ hihostels.com. MAP P.73, POCKET MAP A5. Friendly, quiet and sparkling clean youth hostel, with a small garden. It's also a useful first-night standby if you arrive late by train, as it's just five minutes' walk from the station. You don't need an HI card to stay here, but cardholders get priority. There are a couple of double rooms as well as dorm beds; dorm beds (including breakfast) 73.50dh (hot shower 10dh).

# Atlas Mountains: Imlil

**HOTEL SOLEIL** > ☎ 0524 485622, Ⓦ hotelsoleilimlil.com. The rooms are bright but cosy and mostly en suite at this cheery little place with friendly staff and great views from the terrace. From 200dh half board.

**KASBAH DU TOUBKAL** > ☎ 0524 485611, UK ☎ +44 1883 744392, Ⓦ kasbahdutoubkal.com. The former kasbah of a local *caid* (chief) lovingly restored by British tour company Discover Ltd using local craftsmen, this is Imlil's top offering and indeed its top sight. It starred as the Dalai

Lama's palace in Martin Scorsese's film *Kundun*, but you don't need to be the leader of Tibet to enjoy the beautiful guest rooms or the excellent meals, nor to take advantage of the excursions it offers, on foot or by mule. Even if you don't stay here, it's worth at least popping in for tea on the terrace. Slightly cheaper accommodation from the same firm is available at the nearby *Dar Imlil*. Rates include breakfast, use of the in-house hammam, and a donation towards local community projects. From €168 (1667dh).

**LES ÉTOILES DE TOUBKAL** > ☎ 0524 485618, Ⓦ hotel-etoile-toubkal.com. A reasonable choice in the centre of the village. with en-suite rooms, Berber rugs and a decent restaurant, although the tinted windows mean there's no natural daylight in the rooms. From 314dh

# Atlas Mountains: Setti Fatma

**AU BORD DE L'EAU** > 400m below the taxi stand ☎ 0661 229755, Ⓦ obordelo.com. You'll need to reserve well ahead to bag a room here at Setti Fatma's loveliest hostelry, beneath the road and next to the river, with a small backpackers' room and three suites. The decor in the rooms is well chosen, the tables in the garden are made of old millstones, and the food is absolutely out of this world – home cooking with locally sourced ingredients, often grown on the premises. The backpacker room is 300dh, suites from 400dh.

**HOTEL NAJMA** > 300m below the taxi stand ☎ 0524 485757, Ⓔ najmahotel1 @gmail.com. This hotel functions as a more upmarket annexe for the *Setti Fatma* across the street (the owners are cousins). Rooms are all very simple, though fresh and new, and come in a variety of sizes; all have bathrooms, though not all have outside windows. There are also suites, and a couple of self-catering apartments on the roof (200dh for up to six people). Rate excludes breakfast. 150dh.

**HOTEL-RESTAURANT ASGAOUR** 300m below the taxi stand ☎ 0524 485294, ⓦ asgaour.skyblog.com This bright and friendly little hotel with rooms above its restaurant proudly displays its French guidebook recommendations out front. The rooms are small and plain but clean and carpeted, some en suite, and there's a sunny upper-floor terrace. Heaters are available in winter for 30dh extra. Rates exclude breakfast. From 120dh.

**HOTEL SETTI FATMA** > 350m below the taxi stand ☎ 0524 485509. Formerly known as the *Hotel du Gare* because of its location by the former site of the taxi station, this is one of the oldest hotels in town. Rooms are plain, with shared bathroom facilities, but clean and comfortable; some are older and more basic, others are newer and brighter with a view over the river. There's a restaurant serving food indoors or in the garden. Breakfast excluded. From 70dh.

## Atlas Mountains: Oukaïmeden

**AUBERGE DE L'ANGOUR (CHEZ JUJU)** > ☎ 0524 319005, ⓦ hotelchezjuju.com. There's an old-fashioned, almost country-inn feel about this place on the main road in the centre of the village. It's nice and homely with a decent bar and restaurant; some rooms are fully en suite, but most have just an en-suite shower and a toilet on the landing. Rates exclude breakfast. 900dh.

**CAF REFUGE** > ☎ 0524 319036. Priority is given to Club Alpin Français members at this hostel, which has the only budget accommodation in the village. You stay in a dorm and there are sheets and blankets, but you're advised to bring a sleeping bag nonetheless. Meals are also available. Dorms 170dh (CAF members 80dh).

**HOTEL LE COURCHEVEL** > ☎ 0524 319092, ⓦ lecourchevelouka.com. With its largely wood-clad facade and wood panelling, this place gives an excellent impression of being built entirely out

of timber though it's actually made of concrete. Carpet in all the rooms adds to the warm and cosy feel. There's also a posh restaurant serving Savoy cuisine, and a tapas bar, as well as a hammam and sauna. Open in season only (mid-Nov to April). From 932dh.

## Essaouira

**DAR ADUL** > 63 Rue Touahen ☎ 0524 473910, ⓦ www.daradul.ma. MAP P.94–95. Lashings of whitewash (with maritime blue woodwork) give this French-run riad a bright, airy feel, and help to keep it cool in summer. It has a selection of different-sized rooms – some split-level – and the biggest has a fireplace to keep it warm in winter. From €55 (615dh).

**DAR AL BAHAR** > 1 Rue Touahen ☎ 0524 476831, ⓦ daralbahar .com. MAP P.94–95. Views of the wild ocean crashing against the rocks below, especially from the terrace, plus cool whitewashed rooms, hung with paintings by some of the best local artists, make this riad an excellent choice, though it's a bit tucked away. From €45 (469dh).

**DAR ALOUANE** > 66 Rue Touahen ☎ 0524 476172, ⓦ daralouane.com. MAP P.94–95. This simple and stylish riad has very original, bright, breezy and modern decor in an array of beautiful pastel colours, and thus also goes by the name *La Maison des Couleurs* ("House of Colours"). There's a range of rooms and suites at different prices, some with shared bathrooms but still excellent value. Breakfast excluded. From 200dh.

**DAR NESS** > 1 Rue Khalid Ben el Oualid, just off Place Prince Moulay el Hassan ☎ 0524 476804, ⓦ www .darness-essaouira.com. MAP P.94–95. This is a nineteenth-century house turned into an attractive riad by its French owner, with cool, clean and well-kept rooms, brick floors and jolly little tiled bathrooms. The place is well run, but it does sometimes lack the personal touch that many people expect from a riad. From €53.20 (566dh).

**HOTEL BEAU RIVAGE** > 14 Pl Prince Moulay el Hassan ☏ 0524 475925, ⓦ beaurivage-essaouira.com. MAP P.94–95. A budget hotel that tried to go upmarket but has slid back down again. It has an enviable position right on the main square – which also means that rooms at the front can be a bit noisy at times. There's a variety of charming en-suite rooms, all bright and breezy, the best of them with balconies, but it's not as well-maintained as it might be. From 200dh.

**HOTEL CAP SIM** > 11 Rue Ibn Rochd ☏ 0524 785834, ⓦ hotelcapsim .com. MAP P.94–95. The rooms are a little small at this popular, recently refurbished budget hotel, but they're all clean and bright, some are en suite, and the water is partly solar-heated. The staff are extremely helpful, and there's a fourth-floor sun terrace for catching the rays with a view over the rooftops. From 220dh.

**HOTEL RIAD AL MEDINA** > 9 Rue Attarine ☏ 0524 475907, ⓦ riadalmadina.com. MAP P.94–95. This former palatial mansion, built in 1871, had fallen on hard times by the 1960s and become a budget hotel for hippies. Guests supposedly included Jimi Hendrix (in room 13 according to some stories, room 28 say others), as well as Frank Zappa, the Jefferson Airplane and Cat Stevens. Now refurbished, it has bags of character and helpful staff but it's still rather rustic in some respects (the plumbing can be temperamental for example) and it's relatively expensive for what you get. From 814dh.

**HOTEL SOUIRI** > 37 Rue Attarine ☏ 0524 783094, ⓦ hotelsouiri.com. MAP P.94–95. Deservedly popular and very central, this budget (but not *too* budget) hotel offers a range of rooms, the cheaper ones having shared bathroom facilities. The decor in the rooms is a little bit busy (paint-sponged walls to imitate wallpaper), but homely and cosy. Those at the front are considered the best, though those at the back are quieter. From 320dh.

**LE MÉDINA ESSAOUIRA HOTEL** > Bd Mohammed V ☏ 0524 47900, ⓦ accor .com. MAP P.94–95. This is the most expensive hotel in town by a very long chalk, and it's the place to come if you favour deluxe comforts and amenities over traditional charm and character. Its facilities include a pool, two bars, two restaurants, serving fish and local cuisine, and a thalassotherapy centre (just in case a good, old-fashioned swim in the sea isn't thalassotherapeutic enough). Rooms have a light and airy feel, with a stylish cookies-and-cream colour scheme. Breakfast excluded. 2037dh.

**RIAD BAB ESSAOUIRA** > 35 bis, Bd Moulay Abderrahmane Eddakhil ☏ 0524 785508, ⓦ riad-bab-essaouira .com. This small, well-managed and very stylish riad offers suites only, decorated throughout in cool white with brown and black trimmings and a subtle Afro-Gnaoua theme. Each suite occupies one floor, and includes a sitting room and a bathroom with individual water heater. The rooftop suite has its own small terrace. There's a communal salon and a self-catering kitchen. From €56 (585dh).

**RIAD LE GRAND LARGE** > 2 Rue Oum Rabia ☏ 0524 476886, ⓔ contact@riadlegrandlarge.com. MAP P.94–95. Despite its name, this is a small, cosy place with ten smallish rooms. Staff are lovely, the restaurant is classy, there's a roof-terrace café and it's good value, with reductions off-season. The best room is the one on the roof terrace. €48 (511dh)

**VILLA MAROC** > 10 Rue Abdallah Ben Yassin, just inside the Medina wall near the clocktower ☏ 0524 473147, ⓦ villa-maroc.com. MAP P.94–95. Established long before riads became trendy, this is an upmarket riad made up of two old houses converted into a score of rooms and suites. It's decorated with the finest Moroccan materials and has its own hammam. Though it's accessible only on foot, there are porters on hand to carry your luggage from the car park in Place Orson Welles. Most of the year you will need to book several months ahead to stay here. From 1382dh.

ESSENTIALS

# Arrival

Most visitors arrive in Marrakesh by air, but the night train from Tangier (the "Marrakesh Express") is also a good option, and you can get to Marrakesh by train, bus or shared *grand taxi* from other parts of Morocco too.

## By air

**Menara airport** (☎ 0524 447910) is 4km southwest of town. The arrivals hall has ATMs, and bank kiosks to change money. You won't be stranded even if neither are operating: taxis will accept euros (and sometimes dollars or sterling) at more or less the equivalent dirham rate, or you can have them call by an ATM en route to your destination.

    **Petits taxis** run from in front of the airport terminal. There is an (artificially high) fixed rate of 70dh (110dh at night) from the airport to the Jemaa el Fna or central Guéliz, though taxi drivers may still try to overcharge you – you should not pay above this (it's already more than double what you'd pay on the meter). Shared **grands taxis**, which also wait in front of the airport building, should charge 100dh for up to six passengers for the trip to the Jemaa el Fna, Guéliz and Hivernage. **Bus** #19 (30dh one-way; 50dh return, valid for two weeks) leaves half-hourly (6.30am–9.30pm) from the stop in front of the airport terminal for Place Foucault (by the Koutoubia) and Avenue Mohammed V (Guéliz).

## By train

The **train station** (☎ 0524 449777) is a ten- to fifteen-minute walk from the centre of Guéliz, or a longer walk or bus ride from the Medina; the taxi fare should be around 15dh to the Medina, less to hotels in Guéliz.

Buses #8, #10, #14 and #66 run to Place Foucault, alongside the Jemaa el Fna, across Avenue Hassan II at the corner of Rue Zobeir.

## By bus or shared taxi

The **gare routière** (for long-distance bus services other than the national bus firm CTM, or the train company's Supratours buses) is just outside the walls of the Medina by Bab Doukkala. Most long-distance collective **grands taxis** arriving in Marrakesh terminate immediately behind this bus station, though they may drop you off in front of it on Place el Moura-bitine. You can walk into the centre of Guéliz from the *gare routière* in around ten minutes by following Avenue des Nations Unies (to the right as you exit the bus station, then straight on bearing right). To the Jemaa el Fna it's around 25 minutes: follow the Medina walls (to your left as you exit the bus station) down to Avenue Mohammed V, then turn left. A *petit taxi* is about 10dh to the Jemaa el Fna, less to Guéliz. Alternatively, catch bus #16 from outside the bus station, which runs through the heart of Guéliz, or buses #8, #10, #12, #14, #15, #16, #17 or #66, which stop opposite Bab Doukkala itself (though the bus stop displays only the numbers #11 and #11B) and head south to Place Foucault. **Supratours** services from Essaouira, Agadir and the Western Sahara arrive on Avenue Hassan II next to the train station (accessed via platform 1). **CTM** services stop at their office on Rue Abou Bakr Seddik, two blocks south of Supratours. Shared *grands taxis* from the **High Atlas villages** of Asni, Imlil and Setti Fatma arrive at Place Youssef Tachfine (also called Sidi Mimoun), off Avenue Houman el Fetouaki south of the Koutoubia (see map pp.36–37), which is also served by local bus #25 from Lagarb. Shared taxis from Lagarb arrive nearby, on Rue Ibn Rachid. Coming from the ski resort of Oukaïmeden, unless you charter a taxi, you'll probably have to change vehicles at Lagarb.

Note that on long-distance bus journeys you're expected to tip the **porters** who load your baggage onto buses (5dh – except on CTM, which charges by weight).

# Getting around

Despite its size and the maze of its souks, Marrakesh is not too hard to navigate. Inside the Medina, walking will generally be your best option, partly because most streets are too narrow to navigate in a vehicle, certainly with any ease, and partly because negotiating the Medina on foot – including getting lost a few times – is all part of the Marrakesh experience, and something you shouldn't miss out on. It is true that you could get from, for example, the Jemaa el Fna to the Saadian Tombs in a taxi, but really this is something you are only likely to do if you are not sufficiently fit or able-bodied to manage the journey on foot.

Between the Medina and the Ville Nouvelle, on the other hand, though the distance is certainly not beyond the reach of shanks's pony, you will probably find it more comfortable to take a cab, or even a bus.

## Petits taxis

Other than inside the Medina, the easiest way to get around town is in one of the city's beige **petits taxis**. These take up to three passengers and are equipped with a meter;

if the driver doesn't use it, it's because he intends to overcharge you. Most trips around town (*petits taxis* are not allowed beyond the city limits) should cost around 10–20dh during the day, or 15–30dh at night, when there is a surcharge on the meter price. Special fares apply to and from the airport (see opposite). If you're a lone passenger, it's standard practice for the driver to pick up one or two additional passengers en route, each of whom will pay the full fare for their journey, as will you. There are *petit taxi* ranks at most major intersections in Guéliz, and in the Medina at the junction of Avenue Houman el Fetouaki and Rue Oqba Ben Nafaa, and at the Place des Ferblantiers end of Avenue Houman el Fetouaki.

## Bike rental

An alternative to a *petit taxi* for exploring the more scattered sights, such as the Agdal and Menara gardens or the Palmery, is a **bicycle**, **moped** or **scooter**. You can rent bicycles on Place de la Liberté and a number of roadside locations in Hivernage. Mopeds and scooters from these places will probably not be properly insured, and it is better to rent them from a reputable firm such as **Loc2Roues** on the upper floor of Galerie Élite, 212 Av Mohammed V (☎ 0524 430294, ⓦ loc2roues.com). Expect to pay around 120dh a day for a bicycle, 250–300dh for a moped or scooter.

Getting around town by bike is easy, but be aware that Moroccan drivers are not the world's best. In particular, do not expect them to observe lane discipline, nor to indicate when turning or changing lanes so always exercise particular caution when cycling in town.

## Grands taxis

**Grands taxis** – typically large Mercedes – usually run as shared taxis, taking six passengers (though they're only designed for four) for a fixed price. You'll probably only want to use a *grand taxi* if you're heading to the **Atlas mountains** or to **Essaouira**, but if there are four, five or six of you (too many for a *petit taxi*), you might charter a *grand taxi* for use in town. You'll need to agree the price beforehand.

Shared *grands taxis (taxi collectif)* for most destinations leave from just outside the city walls behind the bus station. When you arrive, ask which vehicle is going to your destination and, unless you want to charter the whole taxi, make clear that you just want individual seats (*une place* for one person, *deux places* for two and so on).

Shared *grands taxis* are fast for journeys out of town, but they are cramped and drivers are prone to speeding and dangerous overtaking.

They have more than their fair share of crashes in a country where the road accident rate is already high. A lot of accidents involve shared *grand taxi* drivers falling asleep at the wheel at night, so you may wish to avoid taking one after dark.

## Calèches

**Calèches** – horse-drawn cabs – line up near the Koutoubia, the El Badi Palace, Place de la Liberté and some of the fancier hotels. They take up to five people and are not much more expensive than *petits taxis* – though be sure to fix the price in advance, particularly if you want a tour of the town. Expect to pay around 150dh an hour, or 200–300dh for a tour round the Medina walls, but you'll need to bargain hard.

## Buses

**City buses** are cheap and efficient. The routes you are most likely to want to use are #1 and #16, which

## Sightseeing bus tour

I f you don't have much time and you want to scoot around Marrakesh's major sights in a day or two, the hop-on hop-off **Marrakech Bus Touristique** could be for you. Using open-top double-deckers, with a commentary in several languages including English, the tour follows two circular routes: the first tours the **Medina and Guéliz**, calling at Place Foucault (for the Jemaa and Koutoubia), Place des Ferblantiers (for the Bahia and El Badi Palaces, plus the Mellah), Bab Agnaou (for the Saadian Tombs) and the Menara gardens; the second tours the **Palmery**, following the Circuit de la Palmeraie, and also calls at the Majorelle Garden.

The Medina/Guéliz bus departs from Place Abdelmoumen Ben Ali in Guéliz and Place Foucault in the Medina every twenty to thirty minutes from 9am till 7pm; the Palmery bus leaves from Place Abdelmoumen Ben Ali hourly 1–5pm. You can get on and off where you like, and **tickets** (145dh for one day, 190dh for two, 30dh and 50dh respectively for disabled passengers) can be bought on board, or from ticket sellers at Place Abdelmoumen Ben Ali or Place Foucault. They are valid for 24 or 48 hours, so even if you start your tour after lunch, you can finish it the following morning.

## Guides

A local guide can help you find things in the Medina, and a good guide can provide some interesting commentary, but you certainly don't need one. Armed with this book and the accompanying map, you can easily find your way around Marrakesh and check out all the sights on your own. Should you want one however, the ONMT (see p.128) can put you in touch. They typically charge around 200–300dh per day. Although it's illegal to work as an unofficial guide, unlicensed guides can be found in the Jemaa el Fna, and will suddenly appear almost anywhere in the Medina if you're seen looking perplexed.

When hiring a guide, be precise about exactly what you want to see and, with an unlicensed guide, agree a fee very clearly at the outset. Whether official or not, most guides will want to steer you into shops which pay them **commission** on anything you buy (added to your shopping bill, of course). Be wary as this commission is not small – official guides quite commonly demand as much as fifty percent. You should therefore make it very clear from the start if you do not want to visit any shops or carpet "museums". Don't be surprised if your guide subsequently loses interest or tries to raise the fee.

run along Avenue Mohammed V between Guéliz and the Koutoubia. Other handy routes include #6 from Place Foucault (by the Koutoubia) via Bab Ighli to the Agdal Gardens, #11 from Place Youssef Tachfine to the Menara gardens and #19 from Place Foucault and Guéliz to the airport. You pay fares to the driver on board.

# Directory A–Z

## Cinemas

In Guéliz, the **Colisée**, alongside the *Café Le Siroua* on Bd Mohammed Zerktouni (☎ 0524 448893), is one of the best in town. In the Medina, there's the **Cinéma Mabrouka** on Rue Bab Agnaou (☎ 0524 443303). **Cinéma Eden** on Rue Riad Zitoun el Jedid was a more downmarket picture house but is now being upgraded as part of a local development.

## Consulates

The **UK Honorary Consulate** is at Borj Menara 2, Immeuble B, 5th Floor, at the northern end of Av Abdelkrim el Khattabi (☎ 0537 633333).Nationalities represented in Rabat include the **US** (☎ 0537 762265), **Canada** (☎ 0537 687400; also representing **Australians**) and **South Africa** (☎ 0537 689159). **Ireland** has a Casablanca consulate (☎ 0522 272721).

## Cookery courses

The **Maison Arabe** (see p.58 & p.108) offers workshops in Moroccan cooking for groups of up to eight people, at 600dh per person. **Amal Restaurant Solidaire** (see p.80) is cheaper, or there's the **Rhode School of Cuisine** (UK ☎ +44 20 7193 1221, US ☎ 1 888 254 1070, ☞ rhodeschoolofcuisine. com), who offer week-long courses from €2145 per person, including villa accommodation in the Palmery and meals on site.

**Police** ☏ 19
**Tourist police** ☏ 0524 384601
**Fire or ambulance** ☏ 15
**SOS Médecins** ☏ 0524 404040

## Crime

Dial ☏ 19 for the **police**. The **tourist police** (*brigade touristique*; ☏ 0524 384601), set up especially to help tourists, are based on the west side of the Jemaa el Fna.

The crime rate in Marrakesh is very low and you are extremely unlikely to be mugged. **Pickpocketing** is more common, especially on crowded buses and in the crowds around performers in the Jemaa el Fna, and you should always keep an eye on your baggage in the train and bus stations. Various little **scams** are practised on tourists, which you may consider harmless; for example, people who ask what you are looking for in the Medina (usually when you are not obviously looking for anything) do so in order to insist on leading you to whatever place you name so that they can then demand payment for it.

Some **women travellers** experience a lot of **sexual harassment** in Marrakesh, while others have little or no trouble. The obvious strategies for getting rid of unwanted attention are the same as you would use at home: appear confident and assured, and you'll avoid a lot of trouble. Avoid physical contact with Moroccan men, even in a manner that would not be considered sexual at home, since it could easily be misunderstood. On the other hand, if a Moroccan man touches you he has definitely crossed the line, and you should not be afraid to **make a scene**. Shouting *shooma!* ("shame on you!") is likely to result in bystanders intervening on your behalf.

## Customs allowances

One litre of wine, one of spirits, and 200 cigarettes or 200g of tobacco for each adult.

## Electricity

The supply is 220v 50Hz. Sockets have two round pins as in Europe. You should be able to find adaptors in Morocco that will take North American plugs (but North American appliances may need a transformer, unless multi-voltage). Adaptors for British and Australasian plugs will need to be brought from home.

## Gay and lesbian travellers

Gay sex between men is illegal in Morocco, and attitudes to it are different from those in the West. A Moroccan who takes the dominant role in gay intercourse may well not consider himself to be indulging in a homosexual act, but the idea of being a passive partner, on the other hand, is virtually taboo. A certain amount of cruising goes on in the crowds of the Jemaa el Fna in the evening. The gay male tourist scene in Marrakesh is growing, and a number of riads are run by gay male couples, but very few by lesbian couples, and there is no perceptible lesbian scene in Marrakesh as yet. The 2014 arrest of a British man and his Moroccan alleged gay lover still underlines the need for discretion.

## Golf

Marrakesh now has half a dozen eighteen-hole golf courses, including: the **Marrakesh Royal Golf Club** (☏ 0524 409828, ⌨ royalgolfmarrakech.com), 5km southeast of town on the old Ouarzazate road, which is Morocco's oldest course, opened in 1923 and once played on by the likes of Churchill, Lloyd George and Eisenhower; the **Palmeraie Golf**

Club (☎ 0524 368766, ⓦ palmgolf clubmarrakech.com), built, as the name suggests, in the Palmery, off the Route de Casablanca, northeast of town; and the **Assoufid Golf Club**, 10km southwest of town on Route Guemassa, beyond the airport (☎ 0525 060770, ⓦ assoufid .com). All courses are open to non-members, with green fees at 400–850dh per day.

## Health

Dr Abdelmajid Ben Tbib, 171 Av Mohammed V, Guéliz (☎ 0524 431030), and Dr Frédéric Reitzer, Immeuble Berdaï (entrance C, 2nd floor, apt 10), at the corner of Av Mohammed V and Av Moulay el Hassan, Guéliz (☎ 0524 439562), are recommended **doctors**. There's also an **emergency call-out service**, SOS Médecins (☎ 0524 404040), which charges 500dh per consultation; the emergency ambulance number is ☎ 15. **Private clinics** accustomed to settling bills with insurance companies include Polyclinique du Sud, at the corner of Rue Yougoslavie and Rue Ibn Aïcha, Guéliz (☎ 0524 447619), and Clinique Yasmine, 12 Rue Ibn Toumert (☎ 0524 433323).

Dr Bennani, on the first floor of 112 Av Mohammed V (☎ 0524 449136), opposite the ONMT office in Guéliz, is a recommended **dentist** and speaks some English.

There are several **pharmacies** along Av Mohammed V; the Pharmacie de la Liberté, just off Pl de la Liberté, is a good one. In the Medina, try Pharmacie de la Place and Pharmacie du Progrés on Rue Bab Agnaou just off the Jemaa el Fna. There's an **all-night pharmacy** (*depot de nuit*) by the Tourist Police on the Jemaa el Fna and another on Rue Khalid Ben Oualid near the fire station in Guéliz. Other late-opening and weekend outlets (*pharmacies de garde*) are listed in pharmacy windows.

## Haggling

Like it or not, for most crafts you buy, you're expected to **haggle**. Contrary to popular belief, there's no magic percentage of the opening price to aim for, but you should always know before you begin how much you want to pay. Start by offering a price much lower than this, and let the shopkeeper argue you up, but not above the price you've decided. If the seller will come down to that, then you have a deal; if not, no damage is done (and you can always think about it and come back the next day). Bear in mind too that, as at an auction, if you state a price and the seller agrees, you are morally obliged to pay, so never let a figure pass your lips that you are not prepared to pay, and don't start haggling for something if you don't really want it.

Haggling is a social activity, and should always be good-natured, never acrimonious, even if you know that the seller is trying to overcharge you outrageously. Theatrics are all part of the game, and buyers' tactics can include pointing to flaws, talking of lower quotes received elsewhere, feigning indifference, or having a friend urge you to leave. Avoid being tricked into raising your bid twice in a row or admitting your estimate of the object's worth (just reply that you've made your offer). If you want to check out the going rates before you shop, visit the Ensemble Artisanal (see p.54) or Entreprise Bouchaib (see p.68), where prices are fixed if a little high.

## Internet

The best place to get online is at the **Moulay Abdeslam Cyber-Park**, on Av Mohammed V opposite the Ensemble Artisanal (Daily 10am–1pm & 2–7pm), which has a super-modern internet office, with fast connections and low rates (5dh/hr). Also, almost the entire park is a free wi-fi zone, with the best connectivity near the fountain in the middle.

Internet cafés (*cybers*, pronounced "sea bear") near the **Jemaa el Fna** include Cyber Internet on the top floor at 34 Rue Ben Marine (daily 9am–midnight; 7dh/hr) and Cyber Internet Teleboutique, 45 Rue des Banques (daily 10am–9pm; 8dh/hr). In **Guéliz**, internet cafés are surprisingly thin on the ground; try Guéliz Info, in a yard behind the old CTM office at 12 Bd Mohammed Zerktouni (Mon–Sat 9am–9pm; 6dh/hr), or Cyber Ahmed, in Passage Ghandoui at 10 Bd Mohammed Zerktouni by La Taverne restaurant (daily 11am–11pm; 6dh/hr).

## Money

Morocco's unit of currency is the **dirham** (dh), which at the time of writing was selling at approximately 15dh for £1, 9.75dh for US$1, 11dh for £1. As with all currencies there are fluctuations, but the dirham has held its own against Western currencies over the last few years. The dirham is divided into 100 **centimes** or francs, and you may find prices written or expressed in centimes rather than dirhams. Confusingly, prices are sometimes quoted in **rials**, one rial being five centimes. Coins of 10, 20 and 50 centimes, and 1, 5 and 10 dirhams are in circulation, along with notes of 20, 25, 50, 100 and 200 dirhams. It is illegal to import or export more than 2000dh, and dirhams are not easily obtainable abroad anyway.

US and Canadian dollars and pounds sterling (Bank of England – not Scottish or Northern Irish notes) are easily exchangeable at Marrakesh **banks**, but **euros** are by far the best hard currency to carry, since they are not only easy to change, but are accepted as cash very widely, at the rate of €1 for 11dh. **Travellers' cheques** are still easy to change, and you can get them replaced if stolen.

The best way to carry your money is in the form of **plastic**, which – if it belongs to the Visa, MasterCard, Cirrus and Plus networks – can be used to withdraw cash from **ATMs** across town. Make sure before you leave home that your cards and PINs will work overseas. You can also settle bills in upmarket hotels, restaurants and tourist shops using MasterCard, Visa or American Express cards. There is a daily limit on ATM withdrawals, usually 4000dh. Using plastic in ATMs gives you better exchange rates than changing cash in banks, but your card issuer may add a transaction fee of as much as 5.5 percent.

The main area for **banks** in the Medina is off the south side of the Jemaa el Fna on Rue Moulay Ismail and Rue Bab Agnaou. In Guéliz, aim for Av Mohammed V between Pl Abdelmoumen Ben Ali and the market. Most major branches have ATMs that will accept foreign cards. **Banking hours** are typically Mon–Fri 8.15am–3.45pm (9.30am–2pm during Ramadan). Most BMCE branches are now open Mon–Fri 9.15am–5.45pm (Ramadan 9.15am–2.30pm), and their branch in the Medina (Rue Moulay Ismail on Pl Foucauld) has a bureau de change open Mon–Fri 9am–9pm, Sat & Sun 9am–1pm & 3–7pm. **Post offices** will also change cash, and there are an increasing number of **private forex bureaux.** There are also a plenty of private foreign exchange bureaux around town, typically open daily 10am–10pm, including one off the Jemaa el Fna on Rue Riad Zitoun el Kedim at Derb Sidi Bouloukat, and one at the Hotel Farouk in Guéliz (see p.113). Out of hours, *Hotel Ali* (see p.104) and *Hotel Central Palace* (see p.105) will change money. The *Hotel Ali* often has the best rates in town in any case.

## Opening hours

**Shops** in the Medina tend to open every day from 9am to 6pm, with some closed for lunch (around 1–3pm), especially on a Friday. In the Ville Nouvelle, shops are more likely to close for lunch, but tend to stay open later, until 7 or 8pm, and to close on Sundays. **Offices** are usually open Monday to Thursday 8.30am to noon and 2.30 to 6.30pm; on Friday their hours are typically 8.30 to 11.30am and 3 to 6.30pm. **Restaurants** generally open between noon and 3pm, and again from 7 to 11pm; only the cheaper places stay open through the afternoon.

All these opening hours change completely during the holy month of **Ramadan** (see p.130 for approximate dates), when Muslims fast from daybreak to nightfall. At this time, shops, offices and banks close early (3–4pm) to allow staff to go home to break the fast. Restaurants may close completely during Ramadan, or open after dusk only, though a couple of places on the Jemaa el Fna will be open through the day to serve tourists.

## Phones

You may well be able to use your **mobile phone** in Marrakesh, though US phones need to be GSM to work abroad. Note that once in Marrakesh you'll pay to receive calls as well as to make them. Prepaid cards from abroad cannot be charged up or replaced locally, but you can get a Moroccan number with a **local SIM** card (20dh plus ID), available, along with top-ups, from *téléboutiques* and offices of Maroc Telecom and Méditel.

The easiest way to make a phone call is to buy a **phonecard** (*télécarte*), available from tobacconists and newsstands in 20dh, 50dh and 100dh denominations. These can be used for local or international calls from public phones all over town (there's a whole army of them by the Jemaa el Fna post office). Another way to make a call is to use a **téléboutique**, where you usually use coins; *téléboutiques* are dotted around town, including one at 65 Rue Bab Agnaou, opposite *Hotel Central Palace*. Calling direct from your hotel room is obviously more convenient, but will cost a lot more.

To **call abroad from Morocco**, dial ☏ 0044 for the UK, ☏ 00353 for Ireland, ☏ 0061 for Australia and ☏ 0064 for New Zealand, followed by the area code (minus the initial zero) and the number. To call North America, dial ☏ 001, then the three-digit area code, then the number. When **calling Marrakesh from abroad**, dial the international access code, then country code for Morocco, ☏ 212, followed by the number – omitting the initial zero.

If you're **calling within Morocco**, note that Moroccan area codes have been scrapped, and that all Moroccan phones, including mobiles, now have a ten-digit number, all digits of which must be dialled. Marrakesh landline numbers begin 0524 (in place of the old 04 area code, which was changed to 044 in 2002, 024 in 2006, and became 0524 in 2009).

## Post

The main **post office** (*la poste* in French, *el boosta* or *el barid* in Arabic) is on Pl 16 Novembre, midway down Av Mohammed V in Guéliz (Mon–Fri 8am–4.15pm, Sat 8.30am–noon for poste restante and full services). Stamps are also sold and money changed Mon–Fri 8am–8pm, Sat 8.30am–6pm. The Medina has a branch post office on the Jemaa el Fna (Mon–Fri 8am–6pm, Sat 10am–6pm), one opposite the Bahia Palace on Rue Riad Zitoun el Jedid (Mon–Fri 8am–4pm), and another in the train station (Mon–Fri 8am–4.15pm).

## Smoking

**Cigarettes** are cheap in Morocco and most men smoke. There are few restrictions on smoking, and those who cannot tolerate others smoking around them will be hard put to find non-smoking areas. On the other hand it is not considered respectable for women to smoke in public, and doing so will look tarty to Moroccans. **Cannabis** is cheap and widely used (dealers offer it to tourists in the back streets south of the Jemaa el Fna), but it is illegal, and buying it lays you open to set-ups and possible arrest.

## Swimming pools

Many hotels allow non-residents to use their pools including the **Grand Hotel Tazi** south of the Jemaa el Fna (100dh) and **Hotel Akabar** (see p.113; 60dh). Handy if you're with kids who hate sightseeing is **Oasiria**, at km4, Route du Barrage, on the Asni/Oumnass road (daily 10am–6pm; 190dh, children under 1.5m and senior citizens 120dh ☎ 0524 380438, ⊛ oasiria.com); it even runs free shuttle buses from town from mid-June to August. The *Palmeraie Golf Palace* hotel runs a more expensive place called **Nikki Beach** (☎ 0663 519992; daily 11.30am–8pm; 300dh) in the Palmery.

## Time

Morocco is on Greenwich Mean Time (GMT/UTC), with daylight saving (GMT+1) from the last Sunday of March until the last Sunday of October, but reverting to GMT during Ramadan until the end of the Aïd el Fitr. The time is the same in Marrakesh as in Britain and Ireland, five hours ahead of the US east coast (EST) and eight ahead of the west coast (PST). In principle, Marrakesh is two hours behind South Africa, eight hours behind Western Australia, ten hours behind eastern Australia, and twelve hours behind New Zealand.

## Tipping

You're expected to tip waiters in cafés (1–2dh per person) and restaurants (5–10dh or so in moderate places, 10–15 percent in upmarket places). Taxi drivers do not expect a tip but always appreciate one of course.

## Tourist information

The **Moroccan National Tourist Office** (Office National Marocain de Tourisme in French or ONMT for short; ⊛ visitmorocco.com) has offices in several Western cities including London (☎ 020 7437 0073, ✉ mnto @morocco-tourism.org.uk), New York (☎ 1 212 221 1583 ✉ info@mnto-usa .org) and Montreal (☎ 1 514 842 8111, ✉ onmt@qc.aira.com). The ONMT office in Marrakesh, also called the **Délégation Régional du Tourisme**, is on Pl Abdelmoumen Ben Ali in Guéliz (Mon–Fri 8.30am–4.30pm; ☎ 0524 436131). For online listings, see the Marrakech Travel Guide website at ⊛ travel marrakech.co.uk.

## Public holidays

Public holidays include: Aid el Kebir and Aid es Seghir (two days each; see p.130 for dates); New Year's Day (Jan 1); Anniversary of the Istiqlal Party's 1944 independence manifesto (Jan 11); Labour Day (May 1); Feast of the Throne (July 30); Allegiance Day (Aug 14); King and People's Revolution Day (Aug 20); King's Birthday and Youth Day (Aug 21); Anniversary of the Green March to occupy the Western Sahara (Nov 6); and Independence Day (Nov 18).

## Travellers with children

Moroccan streets are pretty safe and even quite small children walk to school unaccompanied or play in the street unsupervised. As a parent however, you will encounter one or two difficulties. For example, you won't find **baby changing rooms** in hotels or restaurants, and will have to be discreet if **breastfeeding**. Riads tend to have an adult atmosphere, and some even ban children, so you may want to stay at one of the chain hotels in Hivernage (see p.113–115), which have, apart from anything else, swimming pools. Disposable **nappies** (diapers) are available at supermarkets and some pharmacies. Remember that children are more susceptible than adults to heatstroke and dehydration, so pack a sunhat, and some high-factor **sunscreen**. Wet wipes are also very handy things to take.

## Travellers with disabilities

Marrakesh is not a tremendously accessible city but Moroccans are generally more used to mixing with and helping disabled people than their Western counterparts, and taxis are also a lot more affordable. The Ville Nouvelle is generally easier to negotiate than the Medina, but don't expect kerb ramps at road crossings or other such concessions. There is little wheelchair access to most budget hotels or riads, and wheelchair users may be forced to stay in the chain hotels in Hivernage. Hotels that have rooms adapted for wheelchair users include the *Atlas Medina* (see p.113), the *Ryad Mogador Menara* and the *Sofitel Marrakech* (both p.115), as well as the *Le Médina Essaouira* in Essaouira (see p.117).

## Vegetarian food

Awareness of vegetarianism is slowly increasing, especially in places used to dealing with tourists, but meat stock and animal fat are widely used in cooking, even in dishes that do not contain meat as such, and you may be best off just turning a blind eye to this. Some restaurants around the Jemaa el Fna that are popular with tourists do offer vegetarian versions of couscous and tajine, and the *Earth Café* (see p.40) has vegetarian and vegan food. Otherwise, the cheaper restaurants serve omelettes, salads and sometimes *bisara* (pea soup), with fancier restaurants offering good salads and sometimes pizza. "I'm a vegetarian" is *ana nabaati* in Arabic, or *je suis vegetarien/vegetarienne* in French. You could add: *la akulu lehoum (wala hout)* in Arabic, or *je ne mange aucune sorte de viande (ni poisson)* in French, both meaning "I don't eat any kind of meat (or fish)".

# Festivals and events

Marrakesh's most important celebrations are religious holidays, fixed according to the Islamic lunar calendar. Dates for these in the Western (Gregorian) calendar cannot be predicted exactly as they depend on monthly moon sightings, so they may vary by a day or two from the approximate dates given here.

## MARRAKESH MARATHON

**January** Ⓦ marathon-marrakech.com.
More than 5000 athletes from Morocco and abroad come to run this gruelling but scenic 42km race around the Medina and through the Palmery on the third or fourth Sunday of the month.

## ESSAOUIRA GNAOUA FESTIVAL

**May or June** Ⓦ festival-gnaoua.net.
This annual music festival in Essaouira is held to celebrate the music of the Gnaoua Sufi brother-hood, which originated among slaves brought to Morocco from Senegal and Mali. See p.96.

## FESTIVAL NATIONAL DES ARTS POPULAIRES

**June or July** Ⓦ marrakechfestival.com.
Marrakesh's biggest annual cultural event features performances by musicians and dancers from Morocco and beyond in the El Badi Palace and other venues, plus displays of horsemanship each evening at Bab Jedid.

## RAMADAN

**May and June**
Practising Muslims fast from dawn to sunset in the holy month of Ramadan; the fast is then broken each evening with a meal that traditionally features soup, dates and eggs. Ramadan starts around 6 June 2016, 27 May 2017 and 16 May 2018.

## AID ES SEGHIR

**July or August**
Also called Aid el Fitr, this two-day feast and public holiday celebrates the end of Ramadan. It will be held on approximately 5 July 2016, 25 June 2017 and 15 June 2018.

## SETTI FATMA MOUSSEM

**August**
A four-day annual shindig held in commemoration of a local saint in the Ourika Valley's main village, with a large market, fair, sideshows and Berber and Sufi dancing. See p.90.

## AID EL KEBIR

**September, October or November**
To celebrate the prophet Abraham's willingness to sacrifice his son to God, Muslim families (if they can afford it) buy and slaughter a sheep, which they eat over the next two days – you will see a lot people leading sheep around town in the run-up to the festival. Probable dates (depending on moon sightings) are: 11 Sept 2016, 1 Sept 2017 and 22 Aug 2018.

## MARRAKESH FILM FESTIVAL

**late November or early December**
Ⓦ festivalmarrakech.info.
Marrakesh's big cinematic event is increasingly important on the inter-national circuit, with movies shown at cinemas across town, and on large screens in the El Badi Palace and the Jemaa el Fna. The films shown come from all over the world, but with an emphasis on Moroccan, African and Arab cinema.

# Chronology

**681 AD** > Oqba Ibn Nafi brings Islam to Morocco.

**787** > Moulay Idriss establishes an Arab kingdom in Morocco; Arabs migrate into the country and Arabic becomes the language at court.

**1062–70** > Marrakesh is founded by the Almoravids, a Berber religious fundamentalist movement led by Youssef Ben Tachfine, who makes the new city his capital.

**1126–27** > First city walls constructed.

**1147** > Marrakesh falls to the Almohads, another Berber religious movement, who destroy most Almoravid constructions.

**1172** > Almohads take control of Andalusia (Muslim Spain).

**1184** > Yacoub el Mansour takes the throne, heralding Marrakesh's golden age. Poets and scholars arrive at court.

**1269** > Marrakesh falls to the Merenid dynasty, whose capital is Fez.

**1472** > Wattasid dynasty (formerly viziers to the Merenids) takes power.

**1492** > Fall of last Islamic kingdom in Spain forces Andalusian refugees into Morocco.

**1521** > Marrakesh is taken by a new regime, the Saadians, who make it their capital.

**1557** > First burial at what is to become the Saadian Tombs.

**1558** > Mellah (Jewish quarter) established.

**1578–1603** > Under Ahmed el Mansour, Marrakesh sees a last burst of imperial splendour. El Badi Palace constructed.

**1672** > Alaouite sultan Moulay Ismail takes power and moves the capital to Meknes.

**1792** > The "mad sultan" Moulay Yazid becomes the last person to be buried in the Saadian Tombs.

**1866–67** > Bahia Palace built for Sultan Moulay Hassan's grand vizier Si Moussa.

**1912** > French "protectorate" established. Despite resistance led by local chieftain El Hiba, French forces occupy Marrakesh and begin construction of the Ville Nouvelle.

**1918** > T'hami el Glaoui appointed pasha of Marrakesh by the French colonialists.

**1956** > Morocco becomes independent under Mohammed V, who re-establishes monarchical rule.

**1969** > Jimi Hendrix visits Marrakesh and Essaouira.

**1980s and 90s** > Migration from rural areas swells the city's population. Marrakesh re-establishes itself as Morocco's second biggest city after Casablanca.

**2000s** > Huge rise in tourism, growth of riad industry, expansion of suburbs north and west of town.

**2011** Bomb attack at the *Restaurant Argana* (see p.43).

# Language

The most important language in Marrakesh is **Moroccan Arabic**, as different from the Arabic of the Middle East as Jamaican Patwa is from British or American English. Many Marrakshis speak **Tashelhait** (also called Chleuh), the local Berber language, and most also speak French.

## Pronunciation

In our Arabic transliteration below, we've used **kh** to represent the sound of ch in "loch", and **gh** to represent a gargling sound similar to a French "r". A **q** represents a "k" pronounced in the back of the throat rather than a "kw", and **j** is like the "zh" in Dr Zhivago; **r** should be trilled, as in Spanish. In Arabic words of more than one syllable, the stressed syllable is shown in bold.

## Words and phrases

Even if you learn no other Arabic phrases, it's useful to know the all-purpose greeting, *assalaam aleikum* ("peace to you"); the reply is *waaleikum salaam* ("and to you peace"). When speaking of anything in the future, Moroccans usually say *insha'allah* ("God willing"), and when talking of any kind of good fortune, they say *alhamdulillah* ("praise be to God"). It is normal to respond to these expressions by repeating them. If you really want to impress people, you could try some Tashelhait: "hello" is *manzakin* (with the stress on the second syllable) and "thank you" is *tanmeert*.

Below are some basic Arabic and French vocabulary for everyday communication. You may find it handy to supplement this list with a phrasebook, such as the *Rough Guide French Phrasebook*. Both

Arabic and French use genders, even for inanimate objects, and the word ending varies slightly according to the gender.

| English | Arabic | French |
|---|---|---|
| **BASICS** | | |
| yes | **eyeh**, na**am** | oui |
| no | la | non |
| I/me | ena | moi |
| you (m/f) | en**ta**/en**tee** | vous |
| he/him | **hoo**wa | lui |
| she/her | **hee**ya | elle |
| we/us | neh**noo** | nous |
| they | hoom | ils/elles |
| (very) good | mez**yen** (b**zef**) | (très) bon |
| big | ke**beer** | grand |
| small | se**gheer** | petit |
| old | ke**deem** | vieux |
| new | je**deed** | nouveaux |
| a little | **shwee**ya | un peu |
| a lot | b**zef** | beaucoup |
| open | mah**lul** | ouvert |
| closed | mas**dud** | fermé |
| hello/how's it going? | le **bes**? | ça va? |
| good morning | sbah l'**kheer** | bonjour |
| good evening | msa l'**kheer** | bon soir |
| good night | **lei**la sa**ee**da | bonne nuit |
| goodbye | bise**la**ma | au revoir |
| who...? | sh**koon**...? | qui...? |
| when...? | im**ta**...? | quand...? |
| why...? | a**lash**...? | pourquoi...? |
| how...? | ki**fesh**...? | comment...? |
| which/what...? | sh**noo**...? | quel...? |
| is there...? | kayn...? | est-ce qu'il y a...? |
| do you have...? | **an**dak... /kayn...? | avez-vous...? |
| please | a**fak**/ min **fad**lak *to a man* or a**fik** /min**fad**lik *to a woman* | s'il vous plaît |
| thank you | **shuk**ran | merci |
| ok/agreed | **wa**kha | d'accord |
| that's enough/ that's all | **sa**fee | ça suffit |

| excuse me | ismahlee | excusez-moi |
|---|---|---|
| sorry/I'm very sorry | ismahlee/ ana asif | pardon/je suis désolé |
| let's go | nimsheeyoo | on y va |
| go away | imshee | va t'en |
| I don't understand | mafahemsh | je ne comprends pas |
| do you speak English? (M/F) | takelem/ takelmna ingleesi? | parlez-vous anglais? |

## GETTING AROUND

| where's...? | fayn...? | où est...? |
|---|---|---|
| the airport | el matar | l'aeroport |
| the train station | mahattat el tren | la gare de train |
| the bus station | mahattat el car | la gare routière |
| the bank | el bank | le banque |
| the hospital | el mostashfa | l'hôpital |
| near/far (from here) | qurayab/baeed (min huna) | près/loin (d'ici) |
| left | liseer | à gauche |
| right | limeen | à droit |
| straight ahead | neeshan | tout droit |
| here | hina | ici |
| there | hinak | là |

## ACCOMMODATION

| hotel | funduq | hôtel |
|---|---|---|
| do you have a room? | kayn beet? | avez-vous une chambre? |
| two beds | jooj tlik | deux lits |
| one big bed | wahad tlik kebir | un grand lit |
| shower | doosh | douche |
| hot water | maa skhoona | eau chaud |
| can I see? | mumkin ashoofha? | je peux le voir? |
| key | sarut | clé |

## SHOPPING

| I (don't) want... | ena (mish) bgheet... | je (ne) veux (pas)... |
|---|---|---|
| how much (money)? | shahal (flooss)? | combien (d'argent)? |

| (that's) expensive | (hada) ghalee | (c'est) cher |
|---|---|---|

## NUMBERS

| 0 | sifr | zéro |
|---|---|---|
| 1 | wahad | un |
| 2 | jooj | deux |
| 3 | tlata | trois |
| 4 | arbaa | quatre |
| 5 | khamsa | cinq |
| 6 | sitta | six |
| 7 | sebaa | sept |
| 8 | temanya | huit |
| 9 | tisaoud | neuf |
| 10 | ashra | dix |
| 11 | hadashar | onze |
| 12 | etnashar | douze |
| 13 | talatashar | treize |
| 14 | arbatashar | quatorze |
| 15 | khamstashar | quinze |
| 16 | sittashar | seize |
| 17 | sebatashar | dix-sept |
| 18 | tamantashar | dix-huit |
| 19 | tisatashar | dix-neuf |
| 20 | ashreen | vingt |
| 21 | wahad wa ashreen | vingt-et-un |
| 22 | jooj wa ashreen | vingt-deux |
| 30 | talateen | trente |
| 40 | arbaeen | quarante |
| 50 | khamseen | cinqante |
| 60 | sitteen | soixante |
| 70 | sabaeen | soixante-dix |
| 80 | tamaneen | quatre vingts |
| 90 | tisaeen | quatre-vingt-dix |
| 100 | mia | cent |
| 121 | mia wa wahad wa ashreen | cent vingt-et-un |
| 200 | miateen | deux cents |
| 300 | tolta mia | trois cents |
| 1000 | alf | mille |
| a half | nuss | demi |
| a quarter | roba | quart |

## DAYS AND TIMES

| Monday | nahar el it neen | lundi |
|---|---|---|

133

| Tuesday | nahar et telat | mardi |
| Wednesday | nahar el arbaa | mercredi |
| Thursday | nahar el khemis | jeudi |
| Friday | nahar el jemaa | vendredi |
| Saturday | nahar es sabt | samedi |
| Sunday | nahar el had | dimanche |
| yesterday | imbarih | hier |
| today | el yoom | aujourd'hui |
| tomorrow | gheda | demain |
| what time is it? | shahal fisa'a? | quelle heure est-il? |
| one o'clock | sa'a wahda | une heure |
| 2.15 | jooj wa roba | deux heures et quart |
| 3.30 | tlata wa nuss | trois heures et demi |
| 4.45 | arbaa ila roba | cinq heures moins quart |

## FOOD AND DRINK BASICS

| restaurant | mataam | restaurant |
| breakfast | iftar | petit déjeuner |
| egg | beyd | oeuf |
| butter | zibda | beurre |
| jam | marmalad | confiture |
| cheese | jibna | fromage |
| yoghurt | rayeb | yaourt |
| salad | salata | salade |
| olives | zitoun | olives |
| bread | khobz | pain |
| salt | melha | sel |
| pepper | haroor | piment |
| (without) sugar | (bilesh) sukkar | (sans) sucre |
| the bill | el hisab | l'addition |
| fork | forshaat | fourchette |
| knife | mooss | couteau |
| spoon | mielaqa | cuillère |
| plate | tabseel | assiete |

## MEAT, POULTRY AND FISH

| meat | lahem | viande |
| beef | baqri | boeuf |
| chicken | djaj | poulet |
| lamb | houli | mouton |
| liver | kibda | foie |

| pigeon | hamam | pigeon |
| fish | hout | poisson |
| prawns | qambri | crevettes |

## VEGETABLES

| vegetables | khadrawat | légumes |
| artichoke | qoq | artichaut |
| aubergine | badinjan | aubergine |
| beans | loobia | haricots |
| onions | basal | oignons |
| potatoes | batata | patates |
| tomatoes | mateesha | tomates |

## FRUITS AND NUTS

| almonds | looz | amandes |
| apple | tufah | pomme |
| banana | banan | banane |
| dates | tmer | dattes |
| figs | kermooss | figues |
| grapes | ainab | raisins |
| lemon | limoon | limon |
| melon | battikh | melon |
| orange | limoon | orange |
| pomegranate | rooman | granade |
| prickly pear (cactus fruit) | hendiya | figues de Barbarie |
| strawberry | frowla | fraise |
| watermelon | dellah | pastèque |

## BEVERAGES

| water | maa | de l'eau |
| mineral water | Sidi Ali/Sidi Harazem (brand names) | eau minérale |
| ice | jeleedi | glace |
| ice cream | glace | glace |
| milk | haleeb | lait |
| coffee | qahwa | café |
| coffee with a little milk | nuss nuss | café cassé |
| coffee with plenty of milk | qahwa bi haleeb | café au lait/ café crème |
| tea (with mint/ wormwood [l'absinthe]) | atay (bi nana /sheeba) | thé (à la menthe/ à /sheeba) |
| juice | aseer | jus |
| beer | birra | bière |
| wine | sharab | vin |

| | | |
|---|---|---|
| orange juice | aseer limoon | jus d'orange |
| mixed fruit milkshake | - | jus panache |

## COMMON DISHES AND FOODS

| | |
|---|---|
| bisara | thick pea soup, usually served with olive oil and cumin |
| chakchouka | a vegetable stew not unlike ratatouille, though sometimes containing meat or eggs |
| couscous aux sept legumes | seven-vegetable couscous (often made with meat stock) |
| harira | bean soup, also usually containing pasta and meat |
| kefta | minced meat (usually lamb) |
| loobia | bean stew |
| mechoui | roast lamb |
| merguez | small, spicy dark red sausages, usually grilled over charcoal |
| pastilla | sweet pigeon or chicken pie with cinnamon and filo pastry; a speciality of Fez |
| (pommes) frites | French fries |
| salade Marocaine | salad of tomato and cucumber, finely chopped |
| tajine | a Moroccan casserole cooked over charcoal in a thick ceramic bowl with a conical lid |
| tanjia | a Marrakshi speciality, jugged beef – the term in fact refers to the jug |

## BREADS AND PASTRIES

| | |
|---|---|
| briouats/ doits de Fatima | sweet filo pastry with a savoury filling, a bit like a miniature pastilla |
| briouats au miel | sweet filo pastry envelopes filled with nuts and honey |
| cornes de gazelles (Fr.)/kab el ghazal (Ar.) | marzipan-filled, banana-shaped pastry horns |

| | |
|---|---|
| harsha | flat, leavened griddle bread with a gritty crust, served at cafés for breakfast |
| millefeuille | custard slice |
| msimmen | flat griddle bread made from dough sprinkled with oil, rolled out and folded over several times, rather like an Indian paratha |

## COMMON LOCAL TERMS

| | |
|---|---|
| kif kif/ p'hal p'hal | same thing (I don't mind which) |
| makaynsh mooshkil | no problem |
| sidi | sir, monsieur |

## GLOSSARY

| | |
|---|---|
| bab | gate or door |
| babouche | traditional slipper |
| chaabi | Moroccan popular music (usually folk-derived) |
| dar | house or palace |
| darj w ktarf | (literally, "cheek and shoulder") Almohad architectural design resembling fleur-de-lys |
| gandora | men's cotton garment (equivalent to a kaftan) |
| ginbri | African lute |
| jebel | mountain(s) |
| koubba | dome, and by extension, a tomb with a dome (usually belonging to a marabout) |
| marabout | Sufi saint |
| mihrab | niche in the Mecca-facing wall of a mosque indicating the direction of prayer |
| moussem | popular local festival |
| souk | market |
| tadelakt | super-smooth waterproof plaster glaze traditionally used in hammams |
| thuya | aromatic mahogany-like hardwood from the trunk and rootstock of a Moroccan cypress tree |
| zaouia | Sufi sanctuary (usually around the tomb of a marabout) |
| zellij | geometrical tilework |

## PUBLISHING INFORMATION

This third edition published April 2016 by **Rough Guides Ltd**

80 Strand, London WC2R 0RL

11, Community Centre, Panchsheel Park, New Delhi 110017, India

**Distributed by Penguin Random House**

Penguin Books Ltd, 80 Strand, London WC2R 0RL

Penguin Group (USA) 345 Hudson Street, NY 10014, USA

Penguin Group (Australia) 250 Camberwell Road, Camberwell, Victoria 3124, Australia

Penguin Group (NZ) 67 Apollo Drive, Mairangi Bay, Auckland 1310, New Zealand

Penguin Group (South Africa) Block D, Rosebank Office Park, 181 Jan Smuts Avenue, Parktown North, Gauteng, South Africa 2193

Rough Guides is represented in Canada by

Tourmaline Editions Inc., 662 King Street West, Suite 304, Toronto, Ontario, M5V 1M7

Typeset in Minion and Din to an original design by Henry Iles and Dan May.

Printed and bound in China

© Daniel Jacobs, 2016

Maps © Rough Guides

144pp includes index

A catalogue record for this book is available from the British Library

ISBN 978-0-24123-856-1

The publishers and authors have done their best to ensure the accuracy and currency of all the information in **Pocket Rough Guide Marrakesh**, however, they can accept no responsibility for any loss, injury, or inconvenience sustained by any traveller as a result of information or advice contained in the guide.

1 3 5 7 9 8 6 4 2

## ROUGH GUIDES CREDITS

**Editors:** Payal Sharotri, Helen Abramson

**Layout:** Nikhil Agarwal

**Cartography:** Katie Bennett

**Picture editor:** Michelle Bhatia

**Photographers:** Roger Norum and Natascha Sturny

**Proofreader:** Anita Sach

**Managing editor:** Andy Turner

**Production:** Jimmy Lao

**Cover design:** Nicole Newman, Michelle Bhatia and Nikhil Agarwal

**Editorial assistant:** Freya Godfrey

**Senior pre-press designer:** Dan May

**Publisher:** Keith Drew

**Publishing director:** Georgina Dee

## HELP US UPDATE

We've gone to a lot of effort to ensure that the second edition of the **Pocket Rough Guide Marrakesh** is accurate and up-to-date. However, things change – places get "discovered", opening hours are notoriously fickle, restaurants and rooms raise prices or lower standards. If you feel we've got it wrong or left something out, we'd like to know, and if you can remember the address, the price, the hours, the phone number, so much the better.

Please send your comments with the subject line "**Pocket Rough Guide Marrakesh Update**" to ⓔ mail@roughguides.com. We'll credit all contributions and send a copy of the next edition (or any other Rough Guide if you prefer) for the very best emails.

Find more travel information, connect with fellow travellers and book your trip on ⓦ www .roughguides.com

## PHOTO CREDITS

All images © Rough Guides except the following:
(Key: t-top; c-centre; b-bottom; l-left; r-right)

**Front cover and spine** Fountain in the souk, Medina © Danita Delimont/Getty Images
**Cover flap** Traditional house in the Medina © Age Fotostock/SuperStock; Ben Youssef Medersa © Pixtal/SuperStock; Café Arabe © LOOK Die Bildagentur der Fotografen GmbH/Alamy
**Back cover** Koutoubia Mosque © AWL Images/Gavin Hellier
**p.1** Fabian Von Poser/Robert Harding/Image Broker
**p.2** Giuseppe Masci/Alamy
**p.4** Timothy Allen/Axiom
**p.5** Photolibrary
**p.6** Herve Hughes/Getty Images
**p.8** Emanuele Ciccomartino/Getty Images (c); Daniel Jacobs (b)
**p.10** Hemis/Superstock
**p.12** Herman du Plessis/Getty Images
**p.14** Marco Brivio/Getty Images
**p.15** Hemis/Alamy (t); Photononstop/ Superstock (cl); Marka/Superstock (b)
**p.21** Alamy (tl); Daniel Jacobs (c)
**p.23** Johnny Greig/Alamy
**p.24** Riyad al Moussika
**p.25** Alan Keohane/Riad Star (t); Riad Elizabeth (cl); Elan Fleisher (cr); Riad Kniza (b)
**p.27** Naki Kouyiomtzis/Axiom (tl); Imagebroker/ Alamy (tr); Sofitel Marrakech (c)
**p.28** Robert Harding/Superstock

**p.29** Photononstop/Superstock (tl); Nicholas Pitt/Alamy (tr); Paul Severn/Getty Images (c)
**p.30** Fadel Senna/Getty Images
**p.31** Michelle Garrett/Corbis (cl); Sylvain Grandadam/Robert Harding (cr); Dominique Charriau/Getty Images (bl)
**p.32** Patrick Escudero/Getty Images
**p.54** Joanne Moyes/Alamy
**p.65** AA World travel Libraray/Alamy
**p.67** Svetlana Day/Dreamstime
**p.74** Peter Phipp/Getty Images
**p.76** Marilynn Taylor
**p.81** Grand Café de la Poste
**p.83** Le Jacaranda
**p.85** Arnaud Foltran
**p.86** Naki Kouyioumtzis/PYMCA
**p.87** Sofitel Marrakech
**p.88** Pontino/Alamy
**p.91** Kasbah du Toubkal
**p.92** Image & Stories/Alamy
**p.96** Nick Hanna/Alamy
**p.97** David Kilpatrick/Alamy
**p.98** Daniel Jacobs
**p.99** Danita Delimont/Alamy
**p.100** Nick Hanna/Alamy
**p.101** Nicholas Pitt/Alamy
**p.102** Riad Kniza
**pp.118–119** Peter Adams/Alamy

# Index

Maps are marked in **bold**.

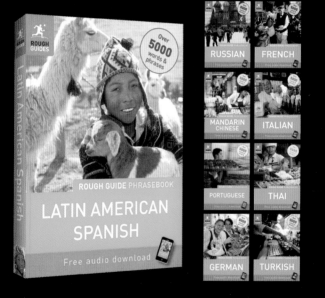

SO NOW WE'VE TOLD YOU
ABOUT THE THINGS NOT TO
MISS, THE BEST PLACES TO
STAY, THE TOP RESTAURANTS,
THE LIVELIEST BARS AND THE
MOST SPECTACULAR SIGHTS,
IT ONLY SEEMS FAIR TO
TELL YOU ABOUT THE BEST
TRAVEL INSURANCE AROUND

WorldNomads.com
*keep travelling safely*

RECOMMENDED BY ROUGH GUIDES